ENERGY MANAGEMENT FOR WRITERS

ENERGY MANAGEMENT FOR WRITERS

A Gamified Approach to Sustainability

Better-Faster Author Success
Book 2

BECCA SYME

For all the authors in the world with a big dream. I want you to be authors for your whole life.

#author4life

ONE

I Still Haven't Learned My Lesson

I DECIDED NOT TO GO HOME FOR CHRISTMAS.

If you know anything about my family, Christmas is The High Holy Holiday. It's the one time of year we all make an effort to be together, no matter what.

In the year this book was written, I'd planned to go on two family trips in December. I was skirting some pretty major burnout from six years of nonstop traveling and coaching.

And even after writing a book on burnout, talking internationally on burnout, and consulting many hundreds of people on their burnout, I still hadn't done the things I needed to do to stop burning out, myself.

Why, you might ask?

Physician, can thou heal thyself?

I mean, it turns out… no. I could not. I still didn't want to do the hard part of recovering from burnout, which is preventing the future burnout. Changing the system so it doesn't run in the burnout cycle. So instead of making choices that were best for my life and biology, I was constantly worried about disappointing people, which would make me ignore the warning signs and keep going.

I still didn't want to talk back to the fear of what would happen if I disappointed people.

What would happen if my family was disappointed in me? Nope, I have to go.

What if that conference organizer believes that I think I'm "too good" for their conference, and that's why I'm saying no? Nope, I have to say yes.

What if the person I'm dating spent the weekend on their own, without me, and thought it meant I didn't like them? Nope, I have to ignore my need to be alone. Just keep swimming.

What would happen if my mom or my sister felt disconnected or hurt because I decided to say no to family time? Nope, I have to let them know how important they are to me.

The weird part is, when I was at the peak of my workaholic phase, I wasn't present at holiday time anyway. I would often be leaving the family gatherings to do coaching sessions, or coming late because I had to travel to Grand Rapids, or ducking out so I could finish that last Patreon post for the month.

But fear isn't logical. My fear-response isn't logically planning out who it's safe to disappoint and who it isn't. It's reacting in the moment to the terror of *what happens if* I disappoint someone.

It is necessary for me to disappoint *someone* when I am running on all cylinders because I've overloaded my plate. Of course, the person I was most used to disappointing was myself. But my family was second on that list, if only because I feel secure in my relationships with them. Which feels awful to say out loud.

Also, I know I'm not alone there. Many of you know this pain from the inside. It's how many of our burnout trajectories work.

So as my family was planning the Christmas holidays this year, and I was making flight and hotel reservations, my stress level mounted. I'd just finished what I was calling my "last official conference," and the people attending had made a wonderful show of thanking me for doing this one last conference.

But I was tired.

I had been going nonstop since my business took off in 2017, and I had burned out so many times, I couldn't count. If you think about what it means to have coached six thousand individual people over the course of ten years... just do that math for a second, knowing I have coached hundreds of them multiple times, and you'll

BECCA SYME

see why I've been burning out. (Although my podcast editor, Nikki, noted it as she was editing our audio podcast for release… *how often are you burning out, Becca?*)

The answer was "every six months," if I was honest. I would be so burned out, I'd either get sick or have to cancel coaching calls, and then I'd have a week or so of recovery, and then get right back to it. I was never slowing the pace, though.

And it wasn't even the pace… it was the fact that the pace didn't refresh me. No amount of resource renewal could help me be refreshed (energetically) by that pace.

We'll talk more about the *why* behind that in a moment, but the key is, I still haven't learned my lesson. I keep trying to change things that aren't too uncomfortable to change (disappointing a few clients who are used to seeing me at a lower price; disappointing a few people who are used to me teaching the introductory class; disappointing a few coaches who are used to me meeting weekly with them to discuss how things are going). But I won't change the stuff that's really uncomfortable.

Because there's fear involved with that kind of big change.

What happens if I quit coaching completely? My business falls apart.

What happens if I stop putting out Quitcast episodes regularly? My reach slows down and I stop growing at the pace I was used to.

What happens if I don't send newsletters regularly? My open rates go down, my conversion rates go down. I stop being top of mind.

All these things impact how I pay my bills, and how my staff and coaches pay their bills. So I haven't touched them.

Until this year.

We're looking at some major re-trenching for 2025, and it's going to be painful probably for everyone involved. But the bottom line was, I had built a house I couldn't live in.

I wanted desperately to be able to live in it. But I'm just not built for that kind of life. And the life I am built for is calling me. It's beckoning. I want to heed that call.

In order to do that, though, I had to disappoint some people. Let down their expectations. It started with saying no to conferences. (Either to conference organizers "no, I'm not speaking," or to clients and friends, "no, I won't be there with you." Both of those were difficult.) Then it included shifting clients to different programs than the ones they were on. And now, it's culminating with me having a very uncomfortable phone call with my family.

I had to acknowledge, I had changed *a lot* in the last year. The ramp down from where I'd been at the peak of busy-ness was pretty significant.

I was finally traveling less. I was finally disconnecting from the industry more. I was finally making margin and ready to take full advantage of it.

Only. I was so burned out from traveling, even the thought of getting on another plane, when I went to make my travel reservations for December, made me want to cry.

Why, oh why, do I have to get backed into such a corner before I'll let myself make a change?

Well, after doing some very intensive work with my Enneagram (no, this isn't an Enneagram book... I'm just telling you how I did the work myself), some under the guidance of Claire Taylor, and some through the reading of Beatrice Chestnut's development books, I could finally confront that fear of disappointing people because I had better tools to do it now. That fear was always present, swimming around just beneath the surface.

What happens if I disappoint them?

Logically, I knew it would be fine. But biologically, I did not. My fear responses kicked up high every time I considered the consequences of that disappointment, and then like a moth to a flame, I would head toward the burn again.

When I confronted that fear... yeah, it still hurt. But I lived through the disappointment. Lived another day.

A loving parent, if they watched their child go through what I had gone through, would say, "darling, Rebecca, please take your margin." So I parented myself in that moment, and made myself say no and set boundaries.

And my family decided to come to me instead of me traveling to them, which was an amazing gift I did not expect. I didn't have to get on a plane. I didn't have to disrupt my life.

At that point, my primary desire was just to be in my own house.

So you might wonder... why am I opening a book about energy management telling you my family woes? Because I still haven't learned my own lesson about burnout. So this book is one part reporting on how I coach people through the effective and sustainable management of their energy. And it's one part me taking accountability for my own choices.

I need this book as much as anyone does. And maybe that's what we always do in the end? We write the thing we most need to hear.

So as I work through this book, I will also be working on my own energy management. Because the in/out dynamic of energy is financial in the way money in/out is financial. There is a resource of energy, and that resource is finite, so how we manage it matters.

How we make more of it.

How we plug the drains that exist.

How we act in a deficit.

How we act in abundance.

This finite-ness means we have to know how to find perspective on our spending and saving of energy. We can't spend without consequence.

We can't spend without expecting the bank to go empty.

We have to plug drains where we can. We have to make an influx of energy when we can.

And when something is really standing in our way of being in alignment, for our own sakes, we have to be willing to reconstruct that part of our lives. Tear out carpeting, knock down walls, trunk old things, toss dangerous things, then rebuild. We are building houses, each of us, with all our decisions, that we're going to have to live in.

Let's make these houses what we want, so we they can sustain us instead of kill us. Let's build our forever homes.

TWO

When You Burn Out

Several people have written books on burnout—one of them is mine. I'm not sure how well it's aged, because I wrote it before the pandemic, but it still seems to help people, so I want to quickly cover the primary metaphor of that book to put context around the financial metaphor of the energy penny as the unit of management for spending and saving energy.

The Pit

When you are headed toward burnout, you are expending more energy than you are replenishing. Some of that energy expending is a systemic response (in that, you aren't always intending to hemorrhage energy, but sometimes the imbalance of stress or the imbalance of expectations causes more of a drain). And some of it is from intentional actions.

Very few people burn out from just working too hard. Most of us burn out because the exchange rate on the way we burn through our energy changes.

If your energy is a penny, and typically, a task takes you one penny, when your stress rises, the exchange rate on that task rises. So much so, it could make even mundane tasks quite expensive to execute.

The more stressed you are, especially the more you're in nervous system activation, the more energy pennies you're burning through and when you've burned through everything you have in the bank, and everything you have in the reserves, you crash into the bottom of the empty pit, trying to scrape pennies from the earth, and finding they are gone.

At the bottom of the pit, you no longer have the ability to make energy the way you used to. The exchange rate is too high, and you're using all the pennies you make in the moment just to survive. Sometimes, even survival is reduced to its lowest state.

You may still have expectations on you that you're required to continue, and in some cases, you can scrape even more reserves out than you thought were there, but eventually, you will hit a place where you just can't continue.

I know we have sayings about "rock bottom," but if you've been in that place, where you can't even get out of bed, you have no energy left, you know there's a bottomer rock.

Not all burnouts are that extreme, of course. Sometimes, we're sitting on a pile of pennies and we can see the very first crack of the bottom of the pit below that, and we stop spending at that breakneck pace to keep ourselves from hitting the actual bottom.

And sometimes we can change the grade of the ascent so we don't careen down there after spending absolutely everything we have. So we level out the crash at the bottom, but we still basically have no reserves left to spend.

That's the pit of burnout. It can feel like a bleak place. Many of us lose business momentum in this place. We can lose health (especially if part of the thing that caused the descent was trying to maintain any health changes or regimens). We can lose friends.

It also takes time and energy to build your way out of the pit, in addition to doing just the normal daily surviving of being human in this world. So it can take even more time than we expect to be in the space of recovery.

And it always takes more time than we want.

The Energy Penny Exchange Rate

If energy can be "made" and "stored" and "spent" and you can be "empty" of energy, then the best metaphor for me to use when I'm trying to help people or coach people to better manage it is going to be a monetary metaphor.

I like so many things about using metaphors to aid in the coaching process, not the least of which is that when we already know how something (like banking) works, then it's easy to translate the same kinds of actions we would use in that instance into the place where we don't have as much facility.

Granted, not everyone has high facility with their finances, so there's always the danger of... are you a good money manager already? But. Most of us (if not all of us) know we should be managing our money, so I'm hopeful that the metaphor will translate in as much as it can.

But the most important part of the energy pennies metaphor for me is the "exchange rate" that can change on you without your knowledge or notice.

In the same way that, when you cross over the border into another country, your "home country" pennies are worth something different in that reality, there is an exchange rate happening with your energy pennies as well.

When your stress level goes up (even for the most mundane things, and especially if you have chemical imbalance of some kind or hormone imbalance of some kind), your energy pennies aren't worth as much as they were when the stress was down.

The thing we see impacted the most, if I'm honest, is stamina. I might be able to do the same work I was doing for a time, but it's a short time. Eventually, the exchange rate catches up with me.

Listen to people who are stressed sometime, and you will hear it. They say, "I don't know why I'm so tired," or "I don't know why I can't do what I could normally do," or "I don't know why I'm cranky these days." You could insert almost any *overwhelm* synonym, and you're going to hear people wonder about why they're feeling it.

Because the causes for those things are invisible. And if we're brutally honest, when we are younger, they don't impact us the way they do as we age. And some of us have gone through not only aging but also chronic illness diagnoses or mental illness diagnoses. Not to mention we are more connected and have more information at our fingertips than ever before, and we are all overwhelmed by it, without knowing it.

We think we like it, but what we like is the hit of dopamine.

Many of us would have a much healthier energy penny exchange just by going through an actual social media detox.

Anything we do and anything that happens to us can impact the energy penny exchange. In both directions, of course. It's also possible to become more efficient or effective at burning energy when your body or system get more into equilibrium. Like an athlete who burns and consumes large amounts of food.

The exchange rate can change in both directions. But most of us are burning at a loss and not realizing it. We're surrounded by pressures and stresses, cares and worries, and we're not able to adequately discharge them because the dopamine production system has told us we need to maintain our connection to email or social media or ads or whatever the stress on the system is that we can't drop or manage.

And of course, that's just one type of stress. That's not even to mention things like the toll of aging or lack of physical health long term. That's not even to mention relational stressors or changes in relationships. It's not even to mention the stress that happens when our expectations aren't met and we can't let go of them.

So many things in life can impact the energy penny exchange, and we often can't see it. But if you meet with me, it's one of the first things I'm listening for. Just how many streams of stress are enacting on your system, and are you able to do anything about them.

Because when we have more peace in our lives, our systems all function better. And when we don't have peace, the systems don't function as well. Psychological peace. (I caveat that because some people thrive in the physical chaos, and that's what brings them psychological peace.)

When the exchange rate rises, and our energy pennies start to dwindle fast, we will eventually hit the bottom of the pit. Fast or slow. But it will happen unless we can slow the descent into the pit enough that we can level out.

The problem is, that almost always takes some major surgery in our lives. Because we aren't burning out from working too much. We're burning out from taking on more work than we can reasonably manage and still expecting ourselves to do it all. We're burning out because we're not being compensated fairly and adequately for the work we are doing.

Yes, absolutely, some of us are burning out from not resting enough, and from that alone, but that is such a tiny percentage of people. Most of us are burning out because of the energy penny exchange rate that we don't see, and we often don't see the sources of the stress, so we're not going after them quickly.

If I could change one thing about our collective unconscious, it would be that the stress sources could be more visible to us so we'd have the data we need to fix them. Because nothing will drain our energy faster, and get us down into the pit faster, than being constantly in stress mode or in stress response.

The Ladder

Once you are in the bottom of that pit, and you address the energy penny exchange rate, you can start the process of recovering. But it's important to know, the process will be long, and there's no guarantee it's going to "feel" like you're recovering, as you are recovering.

There's often been such a drain of resources, your primary job in recovery is *waiting* for the natural recovery process to happen. And that can be very frustrating for many of us who want things to happen faster. But the good news is, you're going to learn patience in this situation, whether you want to or not.

(Because if you don't have the patience required, you're going to end up back in the pit again... so it's not like you can *actually* shortcut the process. The process is the process. It takes as long as it takes.)

However.

I find that being intentional about recovery can help us feel more like a part of the process, and can make the recovery a little easier to wait through, because we feel like we're contributing.

Yes, you can absolutely create energy pennies in the recovery process that will aid in filling the bank back up. But. It's not like you could just do 40 bubble baths in a row or get 40 pedicures, back to back, and the pennies will just magically create the ability for you to burn through them again at a breakneck pace.

It's more that the body and brain will naturally fill the bank back up if we plug the drains. And we can help the energy penny exchange rate stay in our favor by not getting back into stress situations that drain it. Or by doing things to aid the recovery, like.... oh, say... **all the things you wouldn't let yourself do when you were getting into burnout in the first place**?

Yeah, that's typically what we find is the case. Most people, as they burn out, have been keeping themselves from doing the things that naturally relax them. They've been holding off on recreation or rest, and trying to maintain work output expectations for so long, they're forgetting what it felt like to do any of those R&R activities.

So we see a necessity to do some rest and relaxation, for sure (and I don't always mean laying around on the couch... I mean filling the needs you have that aren't getting met).

One of the most important exercises I do with clients in the recovery phase is assessing what their actual needs are (because everyone's needs are different). And if you don't know what needs you have, when you're outside of the burnout cycle or the recovery phase, it will be harder to build the rungs of the ladder to get out of the pit.

But that's what we're going, after we decide to go in the opposite direction of the bottom of the pit. We have to build the ladder from the raw materials around us (one rung might be having a hard conversation with a boss or coworker; one rung might be getting regular massages; one rung might be cutting sugar or social media from the diet; one rung might be regular sexual contact; one rung might be cutting sex out of our diet... everyone is so different).

As we do each of these activities, we are aiding in the process of our natural recovery. But they are the things we've always needed that either we neglected, or we intentionally shut down so we could focus on other things. Or focus on things that felt good, rather than on things that were good for us. (That's a common pattern, by the way... things that "feel" good aren't always good for us in a meta sense.)

But as we recover, we either intentionally or unintentionally build these rungs on a ladder that we can use to climb out of the pit. As we climb, sometimes the progress is slow. Sometimes it's one rung forward, two rungs back. Sometimes it's two rungs forward, one rung back. No matter what, the process takes longer than we want.

However. And this is an important "however" for some of us to latch onto. At some point, the recovery ladder will be complete and you will climb out of that pit, and you'll be back on Recovery Road.

The Road to Recovery

Unfortunately, recovery isn't completely finished when we're out of the pit, because the road will still be at least a little unstable. However, I can tell you what the most common reasons for that instability are, and hopefully that can prepare you for going through it.

Most of the time, we're so worried about burning out again, we're uncertain about how hard to push ourselves. That's the most common "instability" following burnout.

And yes, absolutely, there are times when we think we're on Recovery Road (where we can start letting out the throttle just a bit again), but we're actually still on the ladder and we slip back down. However, if we put percentages on the recovery process, I don't see people slide back down into the pit after they're about 50% recovered unless they go right back to the same lifestyle that caused the burnout, and unless they can replicate the whole descent again.

Because most of the time, burnout doesn't just happen because we're running hot or working too hard, or even just because we have mismatched expectations. There's almost always a precipitating event (something like a crisis or a physical end-of-ability) that tips us all the way down into the pit.

So a good portion of the fear we feel after we're done building the ladder is just caution. I usually encourage people, when they feel 65% recovered, to start pushing themselves at least a little again. That's part of what builds the muscles back after burnout. We have to learn how to let the throttle out.

The other common "bumps" I see on Recovery Road are the pressures of the modern world. The fact that we do still tend to operate at a breakneck pace, and that people tend to have systems that are static around them. So when people start to do a bit more work, and they start to feel like letting the throttle out, and then the system has got them back in its clutches.

They want to run hotter than they're really able to run.

Add to that, there's a good chance our plate size will be smaller when we're in recovery, so we can't load the way we used to without risking some kind of mini shut-down (putting ourselves back on the ladder again and sliding down those rungs).

Managing recovery can be quite a bear, and it's a good idea to think about physical recovery as a model. The way you recover from major surgery. You have to really take it easy on yourself for awhile, as your body knits itself back together, and then you have to start pushing yourself a bit. Muscles need to be built back up. Steps need to be taken.

When you have yourself back on Recovery Road, most of us will forget that we're in recovery after awhile, which can be a blessing. That first feeling of really opening the throttle again to speed down the highway is quite a heady feeling.

We just have to make sure we don't get addicted to the wind in our hair, or we'll end up right back in the pit again. But also. If we do, we will recover from that as well.

Managing Energy Pennies

After recovery (or for some of us, before we burn out), we enter into the phase of "management" of our energy pennies. Many of us will still need to keep an eye on the in/out dynamics of those pennies, just to make sure we're preventing burnout from happening again. And we're going to talk about this process more as the book goes on. (It's what the book is about, after all.)

But I wanted to acknowledge, even after recovery, we still need to be conscious of the in/out dynamics, just so we stay out of the pit as often as we can.

The good news is, once you've burned out, you're more conscious of not wanting to be there again. Assuming we've dealt with the unhealthy drives in us (the ways in which we are motivated by fear), we will have a much easier time.

THREE

Gamifying The Process

As a success coach, I have been working with clients suffering through burnout (and recovery) for many years. I utilize the energy pennies "game" as a way to help those I'm coaching form intention around self-care (in all its iterations).

If you've ever studied gamification, you know there are many reasons to gamify a process. Some involve overcoming resistance (like the writers who use a community or a month-long challenge to get past the inertia of not writing). Some involve making a process fun that isn't currently fun (like those of us who use 4thewords to battle monsters and to get through the laborious process of creating a whole novel). Others use low-stakes as a way to teach (like using video games to help drivers gain hand-eye coordination).

I use gamification as a marker for progress in a process that can feel both inconsistent and worthless at times. Burnout recovery and energy management can lose its impact if we don't have something concrete to wrap our heads around just what we're doing when we set intention around self-care.

We initially ran a Kickstarter to produce a deck of cards, which had some marginal effectiveness, but it's really the concept of the energy pennies in context with the burnout metaphor that makes this worth doing.

When I can internalize the need to make pennies and watch the pennies as they're leaving my bank, then I can gain even marginal awareness about how to help myself live a sustainable life.

This becomes necessary when we live in a world that commodifies everything we do already. Every moment of your life, on some level, is a desired commodity for some corporation or another, and if we don't acknowledge just how valuable our attention, time, and energy are, *someone else will*. And their knowledge of that value will cause us to spend our attention, time, and energy in places that are not helpful for ourselves.

I often use the imperative, "build the house you want to live in" when I'm talking about sustainability both as a coach and as a speaker, to help us understand just how much our daily choices matter in the sustainability of the life we're going to live.

If I'm not paying any attention to the in/out dynamic of my resources (time, attention, energy), then that lack of vigilance can have some pretty catastrophic consequences to my long-term happiness and security.

If I'm not aware of who benefits from my fear, or who benefits from my lack of vigilance, or who benefits from my disconnection, then that lack of awareness can impact trajectories of my entire life.

Again, let me be clear. I'm not encouraging hyper vigilance. For most of us, just a tick higher awareness in the right areas will be important. For most of us, we don't need to be *more* vigilant than we are. We just need to be vigilant about the right things.

Rather than being vigilant about the amount of pain I'm feeling, I acknowledge that some pain is necessary for a good life.

This allows me to say no to advertisers who try to put me into pain (by triggering my fear of missing out, or by triggering my fear of losing, or by triggering my fear of failure) in order to make money from me.

And let's be clear. Those advertisers don't care how sustainable your life is. They don't care if you're spending your last $500 on their product. They only care about meeting the perpetual growth mandated by their investors.

Rather than being vigilant about the amount of uncertainty in the environment around me, I acknowledge that some uncertainty is necessary and some types of uncertainty can be handled when they become a problem.

This allows me to make decisions that are the best for everyone in my life, instead of being tricked into fear response that makes me an easy target for someone's metrics.

(Remember. The goal of doing self-examination is to see if anything in *us* is unsustainable. Not to worry about *anyone else*. Question the premise of your *own* assumptions. Not just those of others.)

But so much of our energy management gets derailed by a lack of awareness of what's actually stealing our energy. So I'm going to put in a plug here for disconnecting more from all forms of influence media or spaces where you're being advertised to. Including your inbox. One of the **first** and **most important** parts of sustainable energy management is being more disconnected from people who want to use your energy for cross purposes.

Even if you might believe you benefit from their purposes.

There's so much stress embedded in the world right now, and even if all we did was try to spend half our days disconnected more, it would be better for our energy.

Try it. Prove me wrong.

The purpose of this game is to put you in more control of your energy, and to give you some simple rubrics to follow that will help you stay at least in awareness of what's happening.

So I want to cover the three types of energy management, and then work through the game itself, because the three types will impact how we play the game.

Then, we'll cover some final steps for how to play, long-term and you'll get an invitation to participate with other authors in this game if you want, though it's not a requirement for playing.

You also don't need the cards to play. The only thing you need is this book. And honestly, some of you will be able to start playing without even finishing this book.

Let's jump into the types so we can get to the playing.

FOUR

Types of Energy Management

It didn't take long coaching authors through the process of burnout recovery to realize that not everyone approached their building-of-their-sustainable-author-life in the same way. And of course, because I also am a specialist in customized productivity, I already wanted to customize burnout recovery.

But I didn't realize that the customization wasn't only in the "number" of energy pennies that a task would take from you or give to you. I also didn't realize, at first, that not all tasks drain people in the same way, and not all tasks replenish. So there wasn't even a way to systematize what "should" be a drain vs. what "should" be a save.

All that work had to be done with the client themselves. And often, I needed them to actually *do* the things before we could determine it. I couldn't just guess for them, and they often couldn't even guess for themselves. We had to actually *do* the things in order to know how they turned out (in terms of "how much" energy it would take or give).

And beyond that, not every client needed to know how much energy it would take or give. Some only needed to know that it was a drain or a save. Would it be a net gain, or a net loss? That's all they needed.

And yet others didn't want any kind of vigilance at all. They just wanted to internalize the *idea* that there was a potential drain or save on the table, and let their intuition guide them into asking the question when it felt necessary.

Between that pattern and the release of our Kickstarter (where we tried to formalize the game into a deck with numbers you could assign to tasks), I found very clear evidence that even the concept of gamification of energy management needed to be customized for people.

Rather than looking for every nuance, though, I'm going to take only the three most relevant patterns that emerged from the research.

Low Vigilance

Mid Vigilance

High Vigilance

That's enough customization for the larger purpose of the game. And then beyond that, I'll give you some suggestions for how to nuance or niche down for yourself. But I'm beginning with the fundamental assumption that you either need low touch, some touch, or high touch, when it comes to management.

Here are how the patterns break down.

Type One: Low Vigilance (Intuition)

You'll know you are low vigilance if, when I start discussing the numbers we can assign to the tasks, you immediately want to close the book.

It sounds like too easy a designation, but the nope-out is so immediate because there's an intuitive part of you that's already keeping track of this on some level. But it's not a level that needs any attention. You may read the book with some interest. You will likely ignore all the numbers and designations.

You may use the lists as ideas for things you could do in the future, and if you ended up with a set of the cards, you might flip through the cards occasionally for ideas.

However. You will not use this as a "game" and will likely not benefit from discussions about how to categorize or how to consciously incorporate the in/out dynamic.

This is because you already do, on some level, have awareness.

Where I see these intuitive energy managers struggle is

in the things they don't know are draining them. So if you're this type of person:

- make sure you're keeping away from negative spaces wherever you can
- make sure you regularly ask if relationships, communities, products, services, people, platforms, activities are serving you
- try staying off social media for a week and see if it makes you feel significantly better
- turn off the news (the news is meant to be checked and not watched)

Your big-picture understanding, or the knowledge of the idea of the bank and the ladder and the pennies will be enough. You'll naturally incorporate things you learn into the management of your daily life if they're helpful. And if they aren't, you'll ignore it.

Type Two: Mid Vigilance (Mostly Subconscious)

You'll know you are Mid Vigilance if you like the idea of energy pennies, but you don't want to use the numbers. Or the numbers don't seem to be helpful for you.

The idea of the game play will be interesting, but not applicable, when we start to talk about "getting to $1 a day" or about the assigning of different numbers to different tasks.

Sometimes, people who are more subconscious in their energy management will eventually want to start attaching value to the numbers, after they internalize how they want to use the system.

Often, these people will start with designating "this is a drain" and "this is a save" first. It's likely that no other designation will be necessary.

You might end up "drawing a card" each day (in the way that, if you had a deck in front of you, you might pick a "save" card to do each day). Or you might keep some of the "save" ideas on a list that you rotate between.

But the highest likelihood is that you won't use the numbers, and it won't matter to you whether or not you hit a particular number of pennies.

I'll have suggestions through the "game" section for Mid-Vigilance adaptations. So you won't need a list of things to remember to do from this chapter. There will be more content for you that's directly applicable coming in the following chapters.

Type Three: High Vigilance (Conscious and Concrete)

This is the type the game was really created for, although I didn't know it at the time. Part of this was necessity (because when I'm trying to help people be more vigilant, but I'm not part of their every day life and I'm not in their house, I need a way to remind them of how to combine the activities so they don't get bored, or so they don't neglect parts of themselves).

But honestly, part of it is how I play the game myself, and this is the part that stalled me out when I was creating this book and this post-Kickstarter product.

I am hypervigilant, by nature, so when I play the game for myself (when I'm actually recovering from burnout), I am conscious of exactly how activities impact me. If I'm not, I will end up focusing on something and there's no one in my house to distract me from that focus. So I need to be more vigilant of my own actions, especially when my life needs the structure that burnout recovery can sometimes require.

So the game was made to be played to its fullest by, unfortunately, the smallest segment of the population who will be using it. It's not a bad thing to be in the smallest use case. But. It did make the customization of this book quite difficult.

I appreciate all of you who hung in there with me.

And now, I can say, if you're this type of person, you'll be excited about the opportunity to have some structure that you can use to help support yourself through burnout recovery.

As we go through the pieces of this game (what all the terms mean and how to play the game), there will be a lot of information for you to get through.

I'm going to encourage you to make lists for yourself, as you're reading, of what activities you want to put on your rotation, and how you want to gamify your days.

Rather than using the cards (which we're no longer producing), you should use lists. Or you can use sticky notes to make your own cards. And frankly, if there's enough interest, we can make a digital version of the cards available as a template. But I'd rather see you make your own system that works for you.

I hope this is helpful, no matter which of the three types you fall into. I know it's helpful in a one-on-one space, because I use it a lot in coaching (more so Type One and Two than Type Three, because the game had such limited availability with the Kickstarter and we're not going to continue to produce it—we have other game ideas that I think will be more helpful in the future). But I'm hoping that even in written form, and even without me to ask questions of you as an individual, this system can be helpful.

So without further ado, let's jump into the Energy Pennies Game.

FIVE

Defining the Terms and Notes Before We Begin The Game

LET'S DEFINE SOME OF THE TERMS WE'RE going to use in this book.

Drains

In energy management, a drain is something that takes energy away and doesn't give it back in a significant enough measure to "make up" for the drain. We will almost always feel drained after these activities. The level of drain is something you will have to decide for yourself. And if you can't quantify exactly, you can use my quantifications and start from there.

Saves

A save will give you energy after you do the activity. You will feel energized by doing it. In fact, often, you'll sort of buzz or bounce with energy after. If you haven't been paying attention to this in the past, I recommend keeping track for a few days with emojis. How do I feel when I finish an activity? And watch for the ones with smiley faces.

Playing Both Drains and Saves (as a Concept)

When I originally wrote these game notes, I was constantly saying, "this is a drain, but I'm going to do it anyway," when I talked about the currency value. So as I'm writing the book, I want to stop and explain something about the Drain cards and the Save cards, in relationship to each other.

The goal of the game is not to "play all the saves and none of the drains." The goal is: when you do a Drain activity, you play the Drain card, even if you don't want to. The goal is to track (for High and Mid Vigilance) what you're doing that drains you, and to compensate for that with things that save you energy, as well.

If that were the goal, you could simply filter out all the Drain cards and not play them. But. You're still doing the draining activities, so in that case, ignoring the Drains wouldn't be helpful to you.

Above all, the goal is helpfulness.

Basically, we want a Net Gain whenever we can (rather than a Net Loss) of energy in the day. But in order to know that, we have to know when something drains us. (Including if it's "something I know is good for me, but which is hard to do, or which I don't like doing.")

But the goal is to play the cards as we live our life, so we can use the Saves to manage the Drains that either have to happen because life has to happen, or that we need to do for self-care or sustainability. (Because some of the drain cards will be things we know are good for us, but which we have significant resistance to doing.)

Like setting boundaries.

Like saying no.

Like stopping work.

Like being vulnerable with your partner.

Like taking a risk.

All those things are a Net Loss, for many of us. But they are worth doing for the care of our selves. So we'll try to play the cards, whenever we are able, and then compensate however we can.

Leaks

A leak has punched a hole in your bank. You're being drained so consistently, over such an amount of time, that recovering that energy is painful. In fact, some of us have leaks that have lasted a majority of our life. I do think that addressing the leaks (either healing the wound that causes them or removing them from our lives) is important whenever we can. But identifying them and doing them as little as possible is necessary. (I recognize we can't always excise the leaks... so at least manage around them.) <3

Energy Penny Exchange Rate

When stress goes up, tasks cost more to execute than they would when stress was down. This is why we so often feel drained from doing "normal" life.

Currency Value

Especially for the **High Vigilance** users, I have included the currency values that I've set, or the rubric for deciding.

In the original game, I made two sets of number designations.

Saves (in cents) were **Green**: 1, 2, 5, 10, 25, 50, 75, and 99.

Drains (in cents) were **Red**: 1, 2, 5, 10, 25, 50, 75, and 99.

Because some of the denominations are quite close to each other, I had a lot of questions about how to tell the difference between a 1 and a 2, or between a 5 and a 10. So if those numbers aren't as easy for you to feel as different, I'd suggest this rubric:

Saves (in cents) as Green: 1, 10, 50, 99.

Drains (in cents) as Red: 1, 10, 50, 99.

The important part of the management is to have enough meaning in the difference that you'll use the designations. If the closer designations of difference don't resonate, use what does.

If you use four, here's how I distinguish between them.

1 cent activities are almost always small things that bring a "hit" of energy, or a hit *to* energy, quickly.

Examples: texting a friend; eating a piece of fruit; taking the pretty drive to work instead of the ugly drive; missing traffic; that first sip of tea or coffee in the morning[1]

10 cent activities are more than the quick hit, and may last a little longer in their "up" or "down" feeling.

Examples: Listening to my audiobook in the morning; Turning on Christmas music to play in the background; Opening the manuscript first in the morning; playing Animal Crossings on my own.

50 cent activities are more noticeable to other people. They're typically the things that even non-vigilant members of our family would notice we get energized from. They also often have some kind of regenerative effect on us. Like they sustain us for a longer time.

Example: talking to the person I'm dating on the phone; playing Animal Crossings with my niece; going to the coffee shop to get work done on the fiction manuscript; cooking a nice meal; going to a sporting event.

99 cent activities are those things where you do them, and the whole day feels worthwhile (or, if it's a drain,

the whole day can sometimes feel like a loss). When drains are 99 cents, they're so significant, it feels almost like "that's all I can do for the day," or "that's all I need for the day."

Examples: Avoiding social media for the day; avoiding sugar for the day; avoiding flour for the day; exercise (although sometimes, this is a net loss for me, if I'm having body pain, and it might be in the drain category rather than the save, some days).

For Mid Vigilance: This might be a second level activity. It might not be what you do first thing with the game. But if you do want to get into the numbers part of the game, you can always start with only two or three numbers first, just to see if you can make a differentiation between "high" and "low" saves and drains.

For Low Vigilance: Ignore this part. :)

Forms of Energy

I have the six "forms" of energy listed here, but if I'm honest, I could have done twenty. As you're keeping your lists, you may decide not to use the forms, and that's totally fine. The designations are arbitrary enough, it's not the most important part of the game. But I also think it's necessary to acknowledge that some of these forms are *easier* for you as an individual, and some of them are instinctively *harder* for you. I made the forms partly to challenge you to make sure you're using all your forms of energy.

A Note About My Style, In The Cards

I know I have a more conversational nonfiction style than some are used to. I often think, as I'm writing, of particular people I'm coaching that I would say *the thing* to. The thing on the card. So you'll see me, occasionally, use first names. That's not to indicate any particular person. It's more to say, "insert your name here, friendo." Because sometimes, we need to hear imperatives with our name attached.

Also, because I am more informal, I'm aware that this might put some of you off, and I do apologize for that. If you think I'm not intelligent because I use *gonna* sometimes, or because I make jokes, then I am definitely not for you.

I have to be myself, at the end of the day.

A Note On Enneagram and Strengths

While I am a certified Strengths coach (trained by Gallup, certified twice—once as a development coach and once as an enterprise coach) and have been coaching in this program for going on eighteen years now, I don't write about Strengths in my nonfiction books.

It's an intensely individualized process, to look at the talents you have that are the strongest in you, and the thing I like the most about Strengths is that they *are* so individualized. In my books, I give more general advice, and then try to tailor based on case studies, rather than on personalities.

Because I use Enneagram for my own development, I may reference it once in awhile, but I am not an Enneagram coach. I have an Enneagram coach. Her name is Claire Taylor and I highly recommend her.

A Note If You Are Not A Writer

I tried to customize this book to writers as much as I could, but I also believe this book is helpful for people who aren't writers. Please insert your own profession, where I've talked about writers. There isn't a lot of difference between how we manage energy when we have a creative profession and when we don't have a creative profession. Where I feel like it's necessary to draw a distinction (because I do coach and consult outside the writing community as well), I will. But mostly, this information is widely applicable.

Whenever I can customize to writers, I will. Whenever I can generalize to all people, I will try. I'd like this book to be accessible to non-writers, especially to spouses or partners of writers, as well as to the publishing community at large.

The Energy Pennies Game

What Are Energy Pennies?

WHEN I FIRST STARTED COACHING, BECAUSE of my pattern-seeking brain, I could often see burnout coming in the far-off distance. And as I coached people through their "hustle" and then watched them skirt the edge of this fulcrum of the burnout pit and tumble in, I started to try to find ways to quantify what I was seeing.

A quick caveat about the concept of Spoons, because this is going to be an obvious question for any one familiar with Spoons.

I was using energy pennies, the bank, the ladder, etc, before I heard about Spoons. If you're not familiar, Spoons are the unit of measurement often used in chronic illness and disability communities for quantifying how much energy a person has for the day —*do I have the Spoons for that*? I want to take a minute, before I dive into the Energy Pennies metaphor, to acknowledge that there is a significant privilege on my part, in the fact that I did not know what Spoons were before I started coaching burnout.

By the time I was far enough into my coaching that I'd come across this unit of measurement, I had to make a decision whether I would adapt to that system or not, and I still will translate my coaching into that language if the person I'm coaching is more comfortable. I don't think my metaphor is any better than Spoons. I just think it's the one I'm used to using. And because I need to focus on drains and saves and "making" more energy, the financial metaphor is the easiest for me to use to communicate the full breadth of the game. I also don't want to co-opt someone else's language.

Thank you for letting me make that statement. It's important to me to acknowledge that I am not the first person to discuss this topic, and for some of you, I won't be the most salient discussion, either. My bottom line goal is to be helpful. So I hope the financial metaphor of this game makes it easy to practice energy management.

For so many of us, quantifying something makes us more aware of it. Especially of how to control it. So as I was coaching in burnout, I started asking clients and friends, "how much did that drain you?"

Compared to how much, say, *reading* filled them up. If you had to quantify which tasks are the most draining, could you? Are you aware of what is a drag on your energy and what isn't?

This was the goal in my early burnout coaching. Awareness of just how much something takes from you. And how often you are doing things that put energy back in.

So it had to be pennies.

Pennies can be spent or saved.

Pennies are so small, we often don't think about them, but they can accumulate (or their drain can accumulate).

Pennies have a worth that is different depending on who is assigning the value.

The basic concept of the energy penny is that our energy is limited (like our bank account) to only what energy we have produced. And that energy will eventually get spent out. The bank will be empty. The goal is to operate with reserves so the bank doesn't get empty.

In terms of currency value, there's a pretty big pain point here.

Each person's "spend" and "save" is different. So not everyone makes energy pennies from the same things, and the same things don't drain people's energy at the same levels.

In other words, I can't just make one set of Energy Pennies activities and say, "for everyone." So I can give guidelines for what works most for the most people. But I cannot tell you what will work for you, with no shadow of doubt. You have to take agency in this game.

You are the master of this game.

How To Manage Energy Pennies

IF YOU THINK ABOUT HOW TINY OF A measurement a penny is, especially in today's world, it takes a long time of saving pennies before you can buy something. And you spend a lot of pennies, likely even every day.

But sometimes, it's the smallest spends that are the most important.

I'll never forget the first time my dad quantified for me how much it cost to leave the lights on. Not just in a "every time you leave the lights on, it costs you X pennies way, but in an over-all-in-your-lifetime-are-there-other-things-you-would-rather-do-with-that-money kind of way.

I noticed that my dad used to go around the house and turn off the lights all the time. In fact, one of his pet peeves has always been that we leave lights on in rooms where we're not using them.

Granted, it's a minuscule amount of money in the moment, but the consistent action of leaving the lights on when you're not in a room is costing money. It will seem small if you take it a day at a time, but when you see how it accumulates...

It made me start turning the lights off.

But it also gave me a very powerful metaphor in my coaching for why it's important to try to make little hits of energy with the extra moments or extra decisions in my life. If I could choose to do something that drains me, versus doing something that fills me... why would I want to choose drain?

And the small size of the drain matters because those are often the decisions we don't see draining us that, like leaving the lights on, over time are depleting us of our energy.

But trying to track things can sometimes be a bear, and I don't want to make it more difficult. So I tried to make a game.

The goal of this game is to become more aware of how you make energy and how you spend it, and to get better at intentionally doing things that give you energy. The goal is to end up in the "positive" to 100 pennies (or more, as you get better at it, or as you have days where you can do more of the "big" things).

But at first, we just want awareness.

So to begin this gamified management system, let's talk about the components. There are six forms of energy that we'll be considering in this game.

Joy, Thought, Spirit, Rest, Courage, and Action.

In this book, at the beginning of each form, I will include a description of the form, how to tell what it feels like (or looks like), and some examples of how it can be utilized.

This book is based on a physical deck of cards we made, but you don't need the deck of cards in order to play the game. You'll just need a notebook or a word or notes doc digitally to start tracking your management.

For High Vigilance Types: I'll include the denominations of pennies I use, for reference, and whenever I can, I'll try to offer guidance about how to decide how many pennies to assign to something. My best suggestion is to do each card one time, and see how you feel while/after doing the card. Assign the numbers for the game based on how you feel after… not on how you think you will feel.

For Mid Vigilance Types: Focus on whether an activity is a "drain" or a "save" for you. And then focus on keeping lists of what resonates for you. If you're able, at some point, to put two or three "amount" designations on, after you've done the initial drain-and-save analysis, that's good. If not, that's also good.

For Low Vigilance Types: Focus on the ideas. I'll try

to give variations on some of the cards so you'll have more ideas to put in your intuitive bank.

You're going to think that some of these behaviors are "too small" to matter, but I've found that the most important parts of energy management are the so-called small behaviors.

Plus, the more depleted you get, the more energy goes to basic system function, and the less you have to spend on non-basic-system-function stuff.

Add to that, the energy penny exchange rate can change when you're in grief, stress, trauma, burnout, illness of any kind, or aging. So what used to make energy pennies doesn't anymore. Or what didn't used to cost anything now costs. Or what used to cost you one penny now costs you ten.

Most of us are confused when our energy management isn't working properly. We think there's something wrong, instead of acknowledging the currency exchange rate, or instead of acknowledging the relative value of pennies, or instead of recognizing that the bank is empty.

We try to solve the wrong problem. (Often, motivation or learning.) Instead of buckling down to prevent drains and increase saves.

Also, making energy pennies can be hard work. It's not always fun. In fact, some of the best energy-penny-producing activities are hard work, like exercising or cleaning. And not everyone gets energy pennies from those activities right away.

But this system is operating behind the scenes at all times, and if we're not aware of it, managing it can be a bear. Too much trial and error for some of us, and instead of doing the management, we end up sitting in bed scrolling on social media just to disassociate.

And you know me, I love a good social media disassociation. But when it becomes the default, that's when I start to worry.

Ultimately, the management of this system is primarily about how much awareness you need to foster for yourself around your energy. Default to the type that resonates the most, to begin with, just to save too much overwhelm. And remember to ignore the parts that aren't for you.

Starting The Game

I'LL ASSUME THAT YOU'RE EITHER PLAYING THE game as it's designed (High Vigilance), adapting the game without the numbers (Mid Vigilance), or reading for ideas (Low Vigilance). So here's how to play the actual game, if you want to.

FIRST: Customize your lists.

There are descriptions the chapters that follow for how to customize the numbers if you'd like to. I'll give you both the designations I use to play the game myself, and also some thoughts about how to set the numbers for yourself if that's what you'd like to do.

I'd suggest making a separate list for Action Pennies, Rest Pennies, Thought Pennies, Spirit Pennies, Joy Pennies, and Courage Pennies. Those are the six forms.

Many of us need to try the activities first, before we can make a designation, so I encourage you to do each one of these activities, and make note of how you felt after.

Do I feel more refreshed? More drained? No change? Better? Worse?

SECOND: Make the lists accessible.

Print them out or keep them near you. This was why I made the deck, originally, so the cards could sit on your desk next to your computer. Granted, you could make cards and print them yourself if you'd like to. But I'm a fan of just using lists instead of spending the time doing that. The goal is to make the reminders accessible for your use.

THIRD: Play the game.

When I play, I keep score in my head. But when I was first learning, I would have a notebook where I wrote down the activities I did, or I'd keep score on scrap paper.

After making the cards, I would deal out the cards as I played them each day (only playing each card once, just to make sure I had variety in my actions). But if you have the lists made in each form (or the general lists of all the drains, vs. all the saves), you'll have the reference points. Keeping score, there, is up to you.

For High Vigilance: I encourage keeping the points score each day and trying to add up your points to make $1 (with the drain activities included). So if you do a drain activity, you count it as a drain, and then you have to make "save" energy to compensate.

This is why familiarity with the deck is important, and adding activities that make the most impact on you (if I've missed something you usually do) is also important.

For Mid Vigilance: I encourage trying to compensate for Drains with some kind of Save activity. Even if you don't have numbers attached, when you know you've done something from the Drain list, then do something from the Save list.

For Low Vigilance: Be on the lookout for your intuitive stops. When you see something in the card descriptions that follow, and it reacts with you in a way that surprises you, take not of that and follow it to its conclusion. That's usually how our intuition reminds us, "you need to stop doing this," or "you need to do more of this." Those might be good lists to keep, if you're going to keep lists. But my guess is, you won't be keeping lists.

For everyone: then we move through all the "cards" in this "deck" (the rest of the book) and read them.

You may not be in the positives, especially on days when you have to do a high number of Drain activities. That is not a loss. It just means it's more important to have a day with a lot of Save activities the next day. There is no losing this game, as long as you keep playing.

Some of you in the Low and Mid Vigilance may want to skim the Pennies Chapters and jump right to "What It

Looks Like to Play The Game" instead, and read on from there, instead of reading every chapter in the "game" section the whole way through.

As soon as you feel overwhelmed (especially with the numbers), start skimming or skipping. You can always come back to it. You bought the book. It's yours. No rush.

FOURTH: Challenge yourself.

Make it complicated by forcing yourself to do every card in one form, or by making yourself choose at random. Maybe you decide to do only Joy Pennies for the day. Or you have a day where you have to do one form at a time (Joy, then Thought, then Spirit, then Courage, etc.). There are so many ways to play this game.

We hope you enjoy!

PART I
Action Pennies

Our bodies are not made for stasis. In fact, when you sit or lay for too long, your body needs maintenance not to go into disrepair. Sometimes, you'll even be at risk for health concerns by being too static.

I'm not suggesting to be active all the time, nor do I believe we can't be healthy and also less active. But I am reminding us that, as much as we might be craving rest in some seasons, we also need the action to keep our bodies (and brains) in motion.

We need something to keep life flowing. Keep blood flowing.

But this form isn't just about things like movement and exercise. It's also about creating momentum. Not all of us are naturally wired to catalyze momentum, so we might need the reminders.

That's what this whole form is for. The reminder that we need to be something other than static. We may not need "active" necessarily, but we need something other than stasis.

So let's dig into the Action Pennies form.

Action Penny 1

Walk to the end of the block and back.

My friend.

Don't think about it. Just get up and do it.

THE PROCESS OF THINKING OFTEN STALLS THE process of action, so I'm starting with action. Leave your static position (take your kindle with you or leave your computer behind), and go to the end of the block and back.

For some of us, this is where our mailboxes are located, so you could set out with a goal of some kind, like picking up the mail. But the main goal is just to regularly get your body moving.

Even when we're wired for thinking, our body still needs movement. In fact, movement can often catalyze thought. So keep an eye on how often you're getting out of your chair or being active in some way. And when you notice you aren't, play this card.

Get up and go. Right now. You think I'm kidding.

Go!

IF THIS IS A SAVE PENNY:

You may not be happy I suggested this, but when you get back from the walk, you will feel more alive than you did before you left.

IF THIS IS A DRAIN PENNY:

You'll feel frustrated or feel nothing. Some of us have very aggressive triggers when it comes to being told to exercise, and I want to acknowledge those. (I have them.) So if this card created angst inside, soothe the angst. Don't just sit in that frustration. Also, because some of us have active injuries or chronic illness, so please adapt this to whatever level of activity makes the most sense for you.

CURRENCY VALUE:

I set my card at a **10 cent Save**. (See the "Defining the Terms" chapter for additional thoughts on setting currency value if you'd like.)

Action Penny 2

Listen to a song that reminds you of a time in your past that you enjoyed.

THIS MIGHT SEEM LIKE A STRANGE suggestion to get in the Action form, but I specifically wanted to catalyze things that didn't always have to involve physical action.

Mental action / stimulation is also important.

Take action to go searching through your music for a song that will remind you of a positive experience in your past. This might take scrolling through or thumbing through old albums and seeing what sparks.

Or you might know the song right now.

Either way, go and listen.

Extra points if the BPM of the song is 120 or above, just to get the heart racing.

My song was "Low" by Flo Rida. It reminds me of the years when I had a really solid friend group around me, and we used to dance a lot together. In fact, just listening to it as I write makes me want to get up and dance.

And more points if the song makes you want to dance.

If this is a Save Penny:

You will feel energized or connected afterward.

If this is a Drain Penny:

You'll feel frustrated or feel nothing.

Currency Value:

I set mine at a **2 cent Save.**

If it makes me get up and dance, then I'd increase it to a **5 cent Save.**

Action Penny 3

Do the YLTW stretch. Put your arms in a Y formation and hold.

Then bend at the elbow to make L shapes and hold.

Then arms straight out at the shoulders in a T and hold.

Then bring your elbows toward your ribcage for a W shape and hold.

ONCE AGAIN, I'M ACKNOWLEDGING THAT NOT all of us can perform physical tasks with equal ease, I've picked something that should be a generally easy stretch for many people. Whatever stretch works best for you, do that.

This stretch is also intended to undo some of the damage of sitting hunched over our laptops or phones all day (and if you're not actively doing something every day to combat that, I highly recommend you play this card every single day).

This stretch in particular is meant to be held for 30 seconds on each pose. Hold the Y for 30, then the L for 30, etc.

Make sure to keep up your deep breathing while you stretch. Two birds and one stone.

IF THIS IS A SAVE PENNY:

You will feel energized or connected afterward.

IF THIS IS A DRAIN PENNY:

You'll feel frustrated or feel nothing.

CURRENCY VALUE:

I set mine at a **1 cent Save**.

Also, this is one of the only cards I'll let myself count more than once in a day, because I sit hunched over my computer so much. It's so important to counterbalance that sitting and hunching whenever we can, so I want to encourage myself to do it more often.

And as a general rule, the only cards I let myself do more than once a day are the 1 cent Saves, because I know I often need a rhythm of those activities to keep me moving throughout the day.

Action Penny 4

Drink a glass of water, George.

Go on. Right now.

THERE'S A JOKE THAT GOES AROUND MY STAFF.
Every time I say, "drink water," they all rejoinder, "but
not too much water." So of course, I have to say...
know what your body needs.[1]

But most of us are not drinking anywhere near as much
water as we need on a daily basis. And so often, we're
trying to fix tiredness problems with caffeine instead of
staying hydrated.

In the same way your plants get tired when you don't
water them, so does your body.

Make sure you're staying hydrated whenever you can.
And drink water before coffee. Please.

Drink water before coffee.

IF THIS IS A SAVE PENNY:

You may feel nothing immediately, but over time, your body will thank you for staying hydrated.

IF THIS IS A DRAIN PENNY:

You'll feel frustrated or feel nothing.

WHERE I SET MINE:

1 cent Save

Action Penny 5

Wake up early tomorrow morning and jump out of bed as quickly as you can.

So much about our daily life is determined by how we wake up in the morning. And I recognize that not all of us are "early to rise" people. That's not what I'm talking about.

I want to see what happens when you get out of bed as quickly as you can in the morning. Just to see.

Some of us are meant for slower paces, so that's not at all a judgment on whether or not we naturally get out of bed quickly. The point is to see what happens.

Do I feel better?

Way too often, we reject advice because we either don't like it, or we think *we won't like it*. But when it has to do with the physical body, I'm always a fan of, "try it for a few days and see what happens."

After running an experiment many years ago (in my 20s), I now know that my days go better when I get out of bed right away instead of lying in bed in the morning.

If you are not the same way, that's still normal. Not everyone is this way. I just want you to *see what happens*. And in general, I'd love it if we could approach all of our energy management with this attitude. Let's try it and see what happens, rather than making assumptions about what *will* happen. (Even if it's happened before.)

Once you try it, this might be a drain penny for you, and if that's the case, I would ignore the advice.

This is especially necessary as an experiment for those of us who have a habit of reaching for our phones in the morning.

Just try this. When you go to sleep at night, imagine how much more alive your body will feel if you start the blood pumping right away. If your tendency is to assume it will be painful, try thinking *let me just see what happens... let me suspend my judgment*. Maybe even imagine how great it would feel if it worked.

Try that and see if it makes a difference.

If this is a Save Penny:

You'll feel energized afterward.

If this is a Drain Penny:

You'll feel frustrated or feel nothing.

Where I set mine:

5 cent Save

(Side note: when I wrote the game notes originally, I set this as a 1 cent Drain and I'll acknowledge, it was much harder to do then that it is now. Right now, it's the Fall, which is my favorite time of year, and when I wrote the notes originally, it was the Winter, which is categorically a harder time for me to have action catalyst. So just a reminder that the denominations of your currency value can always change, if the environment, circumstances, biology, etc., also change.)

Action Penny 6

If you have a bicycle, pull it out and ride it. If you have sporting equipment, throw a ball around. Play.

I'M THE MOST INTERESTED IN THE "PLAY" word, here, rather than the "exercise" word. In fact, I'm almost zero interested in where your heart rate is (unless it's in a danger zone, and then, take care of yourself).

But I want to see you do something that will feel like play. I suggested the bicycle because, for many of us who are not chronic exercisers in adulthood, we might still associate bikes and sporting equipment with childhood play.

And while I don't necessarily need the play to feel childish, I do want it to feel playful. So if bikes aren't the thing that make you feel playful, go ahead and pick another more playful activity.

If this is a Save Penny:

You'll feel energized afterward.

If this is a Drain Penny:

You'll feel frustrated or feel nothing.

Where I set mine:

2 cent Drain

Action Penny 7

Flex your feet and ankles, as you are able, while you are sitting or laying down.

MANY OF THESE ACTION CARDS ARE MEANT TO get the blood flowing, so this is another one where I'm not really interested in "exercise" per se. I'm the most interested in your blood flowing.

And while I would love to see us walking stairs regularly, just to keep our body musculature intact, I'm the most interested in blood flow. So something like flexing feet and pointing toes while sitting or doing ankle dexterity excrcises are more important.

We need to remember to do things throughout the day that keep our bodies alive. Too many of us are disconnected from what our bodies are feeling (especially because they might be in pain, so that's reasonable). So I want just a little more awareness of blood flow.

If this is a Save Penny:

You'll feel energized afterward.

If this is a Drain Penny:

You'll feel frustrated or feel nothing.

Where I set mine:

1 cent Save

(This is another one where I'll let myself play it multiple times during the day, just to keep my body moving and blood flowing.)

Action Penny 8

Hug someone.

Or hold hands. Or just sit in the same space.

THIS IS PRIMARILY A "NERVOUS SYSTEM regulation" activity, for me. I'm less interested in the relational aspects of this, and more interested in the physical impact on our nervous system.

During the pandemic, too many of us were more isolated than we should have been (for the health of our body and psyche). And lots of us still haven't counteracted the negative impact.

My goal, with this card, would be to see you play it as often as possible. Many of us are touch starved, and I don't mean that in a sexual way (although for some of us, it can also be sexual). I mean having physical human contact.

Find someone to hug. Or hold hands with. Or sit next to.

And obviously, consent is key here. So don't hug random people or unwilling people. And never touch unwilling people. But if you can find someone who wants to hug you back (they also likely need the touch... almost everyone is showing signs of being touch-starved).

That's your action card. Hug.

IF THIS IS A SAVE PENNY:

You'll feel calm or heart-warm afterward.

IF THIS IS A DRAIN PENNY:

You'll feel frustrated or feel nothing. Not all of us are energized by physical touch, and this is important to know about yourself. Completely normal. Good to know.

WHERE I SET MINE:

25 cent Save

(And even as I wrote this, I could feel the truth in my body that for me, I would like to hug some people more than others, so there are particular people where a hug from them would be 99 cents. One person in particular, who I don't get to hug. So. That's also important to pay attention to.)

IF THIS IS A LEAK:

Some of us have trauma that's associated with touch. If that's the case, as always, ignore me. <3

Action Penny 9

Eat a vegetable or a piece of fruit. (Try a new one
if you're bored.)

I'm TRYING HARD NOT TO TOUCH TOO MANY
trigger-y health things in this book. And this is less
about monitoring what you eat, and more about
making sure you're adding in things that will make you
feel better.

Pick a vegetable or a piece of fruit that you like and eat
that.

I also added the "try a new one if you're bored" because
I've got a high need for "new and different" in my
personality, and I've found that trying new fruits and
vegetables gives me a boost.

Every time I go to a new state or country, I always want to try the food there, and I specifically look for things I can't get where I live, because I want to sample all the variety.

In fact, I now have a running list of all the fruits I haven't tried yet, and as soon as I'm done with all 50 states, I'm going to set out on the fruit and vegetable trying excursions. (I'm going to have to hit countries I haven't been to in order to find these things, anyway. So. I'm excited.)

Hopefully this will be a fun card for you. It's ok, too, if it isn't.

IF THIS IS A SAVE PENNY:

You'll feel calm or happy afterward.

IF THIS IS A DRAIN PENNY:

You'll feel frustrated or feel nothing.

WHERE I SET MINE:

2 cent Save

(Although if I have to leave the house to do it, rather than having the fruit already in my house, I'm probably not going to count it as a Save unless I have the time and inclination to leave the house already.)

Action Penny 10

Do your laundry, Kevin. Or switch the laundry, Kevin. Or fold the laundry, Kevin... you pick.

I KNOW, I KNOW... I'M NOT GOING TO SAY anything about this card, because I don't want anyone to feel bad for not being vigilant about laundry. Laundry vigilance isn't righteous. This was just to catalyze something that many of us need the reminder to do.

I hope it helps.

IF THIS IS A SAVE PENNY:

You'll feel accomplished afterward.

. . .

IF THIS IS A DRAIN PENNY:

You'll feel frustrated or feel nothing.

WHERE I SET MINE:

10 cent Drain - I do not like laundry. But it needs doing.

Optional Additional Action Pennies

I HAVE BEEN COLLECTING SOME ACTIVITIES that I think you might want to consider adding to your action pennies list, but which I did not include on the printed cards. So here are some thoughts for where you could add other cards to your own deck.

Some of these tasks require spending money, so I'm acknowledging ahead of time that often, in our culture, health is a privilege. If at all possible, when you can't afford something, try to find someone in your life who's willing to support you in the way you need. (And I know that support is a privilege, too.) But these are just a jumping-off point for more ideas.

- Buy a foam roller and stretch your back regularly.
- Stand up and touch your toes.
- Pick up the clutter around you.
- Organize those papers.

- Go get your mail.
- Open your mail and pay bills.
- Recycle boxes.
- Take out the trash.
- Clean the refrigerator.
- Clean the bathrooms.
- Organize your office.
- Unpack boxes.
- Crochet or knit.
- Do martial arts or another active self-driven activity.
- Rake your yard.
- Mow the lawn.
- Hire someone to mow your lawn or rake your yard.
- Water your plants.

Anything that makes you feel energized, enthusiastic, or active is what we're looking for in the Action Pennies form. Blood flow.

PART II

Rest Pennies

This hopefully won't be controversial, as there are **many** books on the market now about the importance of rest.

Most of us need more rest.

But not just rest in a physical sense. We also need rest from the world. We need breaks from knowing what's going on in the entire globe. We need rest mentally as much as we need physical rest.

Our eyes and heads are often crying out for us to take more rest from screens, and we're often not listening (or we think we can't). So once again, I'm going to encourage the making of pennies without screens whenever you can.

Rest Penny 1

The thing you volunteered for, but you want to get out of it? Cancel right now, Susan. Tell them Becca made you.

I'M NOT PULLING PUNCHES IN THIS BOOK, even on myself. I have been meaning to cancel something I'd volunteered for, long ago, and I keep putting it off because I know it's going to be painful to get out of. They were counting on me being there.

But also. My health is more important, and right now, that trip will cost me too much (not just financially, but spiritually, physically, and emotionally). There are other people who can be present in that place. Not everywhere is my job.

When we are asked to volunteer, we often become

more aware of the other person's feelings than we are of our own.qa

The more of a parent pleaser we were as a kid, the more likely we are to get triggered into saying yes to things we don't want to say yes to, especially if our personality also aligns with things like Gretchen Rubin's Obligers, or are high Stability in the DISC.

So if you find yourself saying yes to things all the time, we set the task of learning to say no.

Saying no doesn't just happen.

In fact, I think the "No is a complete sentence" phrasing does more harm than good. Because we're convinced of the logic when we read it on Instagram, but when it comes time to actually say no to the person in front of us (or to the opportunity we want), we struggle.

Something else is more important, but we don't know that. We think, "but I know this: 'no is a complete sentence,' so why don't I say no?"

When someone asks you to do something, your internal fear of disappointing people kicks in, and the fear is louder. Or your childhood fear of not being lovable. Or your old-coded fear of not being safe. None of these fears will allow you to either say no, or to not try to give reasons or excuses for why you're saying no.

Something is making you say *yes* in the moment.

The way to counteract that is to figure out where it's coming from, heal that place (or soothe that fear, or regulate that nervous system), and that will likely take some work.

1. Are we feeling their desire for us to say yes, and is that desire triggering a "must please" response? If it is, there's likely a need for us to do some work (maybe some therapy) around the okay-ness with disappointing people. If you have training from childhood around being made to feel like it was your job to please the adults around you, there's a good likelihood you are going into survival mode when people want something from you and you don't realize it.

In that case, nervous system work will help, but you'll have to practice it regularly.

The word "no" doesn't just appear. We have to invite it.

2. Are we feeling an intense excitement about taking the opportunity, or feeling fear about saying no (it might hamper my career)? If it is, and this is a personality trait, we will need to burn out (maybe multiple times) to learn. That's usually the only thing that will really make us take the fear work seriously. Paying consequences for over-commitment. Especially because that excess of commitment will have consequences.

The main issue with this kind of fear is that we think it's enthusiasm. We like opportunity, we tell ourselves.

We can do just a little more work, we tell ourselves. But really, there's a lion nipping at our heels.

3. Are we afraid of missing out? If we are, I wish I had better news in this arena, but no matter how hard we work on FOMO, unless we aggressively go after nervous system regulation as a skill, we're unlikely to conquer FOMO simply by being aware of it. In fact, on some level, the colloquial obsession with FOMO is making it worse, and not better. We're now talking about missing out so much, we've normalized the fear response, rather than the soothe.

Have you ever heard the elephant conundrum? When I tell you not to think about an elephant, you're now thinking of an elephant because I brought it up?

FOMO is similar.

Many of us make FOMO worse by trying to think or learn about FOMO, rather than attacking it at the source, as the survival mechanism skill it is. When you're afraid, solve the fear first. Don't try to talk to it. It can't listen. It has to be shown that you're okay.

Fear isn't logical. (I mean, it can't hear logic. The original coding of the fear makes all kinds of sense. But the fear won't disappear just because you know, logically, you shouldn't need this thing.) It's biological.

Huge fan of Sarah Baldwin, if you're looking for resources here. She has a few great episodes on the Mark Groves podcast that are pretty seminal for quick teaching about nervous system regulation. I highly recommend checking her out if this is a struggle for you.

If this is a Save Penny:

You will feel heart-warm during and afterward.

If this is a Drain Penny:

You'll feel frustrated or scared. Depending on your background, this might be a card that requires therapeutic support, or some on-your-own personal work (like Sarah Baldwin or Thais Gibson).

Where I set mine:

25 cent Drain

Rest Penny 2

Gather all the pillows in your house into one spot and sit in them. Make yourself comfortable and stay for five minutes.

YES, I MEAN ALL THE PILLOWS, JASON.

(Jason, Jason, Jason...) (said in a Jimmy Rees voice)

Gather all the pillows and sit in them. Get comfortable, and stay there for five minutes. Maybe longer.

IF THIS IS A SAVE PENNY:

You will feel heart-warm and safe during and afterward.

. . .

IF THIS IS A DRAIN PENNY:

You'll feel frustrated or feel nothing.

WHERE I SET MINE:

1 cent Save (I do this in my bed, so I can really "sink in" and feel all the comfort around me)

Rest Penny 3

Close your eyes and practice box breathing.

Breathe in for four.

Hold for four.

Breathe out for four.

Hold for four.

THE BENEFITS OF INTENTIONAL BREATH exercises have been well-documented, so I'm not going to exhaust them. Let me just say, from the perspective of someone who has been doing a lot of box breathing lately, the difference is pretty visible for me.

It's one of the tools for nervous system regulation. But it needs to be done regularly.

And when I do one of these, I try to do at least four.

You could also do the 30-30-30, where you basically do this practice, but 30 times in a row, then hold as long as you can on the breath out, then hold as long as you can on the breath in, then repeat the process twice more.

IF THIS IS A SAVE PENNY:

You will feel energized afterward.

IF THIS IS A DRAIN PENNY:

You'll feel frustrated or feel nothing. Some of us have pretty significant breathing issues, and if this agitates those, ignore me with this card, completely.

WHERE I SET MINE:

2 cent Save

Rest Penny 4

Go to bed early tonight, Jen. Shut down your tech at least an hour before bedtime.

I KNOW, I KNOW. NONE OF US WANT TO HEAR that if we want better rest, we need to monitor our phone addictions. (And many of us get uncomfortable really fast when I use the word "addiction" to describe how we are with our phones. That's the addicted part of us scared someone will take away their comfort.)

So this card, especially, I want us to try doing.

No phones at least an hour before bedtime. (And I don't mean an hour before you think you'll fall asleep... I mean an hour before you get into bed.)

I would prefer if you had no screens at all in the bedroom. Just to show yourself what will happen if you have no screens in the bedroom. In fact, I should be clear... I don't mean shut down the phone but keep the iPad on. I don't mean shut down the phone but keep on the backlit Kindle. I don't mean shut down the phone but watch the TV.

Deal with your boredom.

Do some deep breathing. Do some focused meditation. Soothe the part of you that wants to see what's happening on TikTok. (Again, the nervous system regulation tactics are so important.)

But for the purpose of rest, please do this card. Not only do I think it will help for better rest, but I also believe that it will help with things like clarity of thought, depth of security. Yes, it will be difficult, especially at first. Those parts of our brain that are used to getting the neurochemicals they've been getting for years don't want to stop getting them. Yes, there will be pain. But if it could help you to feel less overwhelmed, less tired, less worried, less fractured... I think it's worth the short-term pain for long-term gain.

(I just don't think we realize how the "race to the bottom of the brain stem" with the goal of tech companies getting our money has created a situation where we're all activated all the time, in the way we would be activated if we were in danger or arousal. That's a lot of stress on the body. Ok, I'm done now. But. Just try this.)

. . .

IF THIS IS A SAVE PENNY:

You will feel rested afterward.

IF THIS IS A DRAIN PENNY:

You'll feel frustrated or feel nothing. (And again, it might be a drain for a few days, but you should eventually see an ability to relax better, if this was a problem for your energy.)

WHERE I SET MINE:

10 cent Drain

At first, this is absolutely a drain card for me. But then, after I do it for awhile, it starts to get into "Save" territory. I definitely do not like doing it, but I know how important it is.

Rest Penny 5

Wake up late tomorrow morning. Later than you want to. Later than is comfortable.

ODDLY, I DID THIS LAST NIGHT WITHOUT meaning to. I intentionally didn't set my alarm because I'd been up late, and let myself sleep until my body woke me up. That's sort of the goal of this card.

To let your body decide when it's going to wake up.

I know this might cause problems for some of us (people needing us to be places, etc.) so obviously, use discretion doing this card. But I also want you to see what happens when you do it. Is the feeling of being a bit more rested worth it? (No matter what your assumptions are about it.)

So much of what we do is based on anticipated outcomes. But we can be wrong about those anticipations. So often.

Just test the concept. Question the premise.

If this is a Save Penny:

You will feel rested afterward.

If this is a Drain Penny:

You'll feel frustrated or feel nothing. (And again, it might be a drain for a few days, but you should eventually see an ability to relax better, if this was a problem for your energy.)

Where I set mine:

5 cent Save

Rest Penny 6

Read a book, Jason.

Go on.

A BOOK. ANY BOOK. NO MATTER THE complexity or subject matter. Anything that will put your brain to rest.

IF THIS IS A SAVE PENNY:

You will feel rested afterward.

IF THIS IS A DRAIN PENNY:

You'll feel frustrated or feel nothing.

.   .   .

Where I set mine:

2 cent Save (could be more, depending on the book)

Rest Penny 7

Lie on the ground and stare at the ceiling. Extra points if this is outside, staring at the clouds or the sky.

THIS HAS A LOT TO DO WITH RESTING OUR eyes, especially making sure our eyes aren't staring at screens all day. In fact, if I could, I'd make everyone do this every day. No matter their age.

And of course, as always, modify for your physical abilities (not everyone's able to get up and down off the ground easily).

If you've never (or not recently) laid down outside and stared at the clouds or the sky, I do recommend this.

IF THIS IS A SAVE PENNY:

You will feel rested afterward.

IF THIS IS A DRAIN PENNY:

You'll feel frustrated or feel nothing.

WHERE I SET MINE:

1 cent Save

Rest Penny 8

Play a video game. Of any kind, for any length of time.

THERE HAS BEEN SO MUCH WORK DONE recently (academically) in understanding the benefits of video games, so I hope, if you're a gamer, you already feel like it's ok to have the hobby you have. Additionally, video games can be really good for us.

(Again, the issue is when we use them too aggressively to disassociate and never deal with our adult responsibilities... that's a separate experience all together.)

But in terms of beneficial rest exercise, the right video games can rest our brains. So I want you to try one, if you haven't before, just to see what the experience will be like for your brain.

Personally, I find the most rest when I'm playing games I've played before. (This isn't about stimulation, although games can provide that as well.) So when I need to rest my brain, I play Animal Crossings New Horizons (ACNH).

I also know several attentive-brain friends who rest more playing new games. Again, it's about resting the brain from other activities.

Play this card only one time a day for points.

IF THIS IS A SAVE PENNY:

You will feel rested afterward.

IF THIS IS A DRAIN PENNY:

You'll feel frustrated or feel nothing.

WHERE I SET MINE:

1 cent Save

Rest Penny 9

Take a day fully off social media.

Fully, my friend.

Some of you are getting frustrated with the amount of time I'm spending talking about social media because you already don't like it and don't want to be on it. And I get that.

Many studies have been done on the ubiquity of social media. And of the people I coach toward greater productivity, the one thing that makes the most difference is not getting on social media in the morning. So I apologize for how hard I'm hitting this. The coding to encourage us toward this activity is deep.

So if you're a person who already doesn't do social

media, you're getting the pennies of rest for your brain already.

But if you are a person who spends every single day (especially all day) on social media, please, my friend, take a whole day off.

And maybe make that a regular practice.

If you haven't seen Tristan Harris talk about the "race to the bottom of the brain stem" before, I highly recommend you check out his discussions on why the development of social media (unchecked) has not been good for our well-being. But because we're wired for survival, not happiness, we're using things like technology and digital connections on a survival level without being aware of it.

My goal is just awareness. And to give us back some modicum of control. Even just waiting half the day to go on social media would be better than reaching for your phone first thing.

I know, I know. I'll stop now.

IF THIS IS A SAVE PENNY:

You will feel rested afterward.

IF THIS IS A DRAIN PENNY:

You'll feel frustrated or feel nothing.

WHERE I SET MINE:

5 cent Save

Rest Penny 10

Limit your screen time today and spend more time looking at physical objects and real people.

EVEN IF YOU DON'T ACTUALLY TAKE BREAK-breaks from tech (like a day or two days, etc.), consider taking a short break every hour or every 45 minutes. Stop looking at the screen. Look at something across the room. Look at a plant or a tree. Look at a person or an animal.

Focus on something that isn't two-dimensional.

Sometimes, the two-dimensional world feels too real, and the three-dimensional world doesn't feel real enough.

Rest your eyeballs.

. . .

If this is a Save Penny:

You will feel relieved afterward.

If this is a Drain Penny:

You'll feel nothing.

Where I set mine:

1 cent Save

Optional Additional Rest Pennies

I HAVE BEEN COLLECTING SOME ACTIVITIES that I think you might want to consider adding to your rest pennies list, but which I did not include on the printed cards. So here are some thoughts for where you could add other cards to your own deck.

Some of these tasks require spending money, so I'm acknowledging ahead of time that often, in our culture, rest is a privilege. If at all possible, when you can't afford something, try to find someone in your life who's willing to support you in the way you need. (And I know that support is a privilege, too.) But these are just a jumping-off point for more ideas.

- Take a break from a relationship.
- Book a spa day or massage.
- Hire a housekeeper.
- Pay someone to pick up and drop off your children to school.

- Spend a whole day on the couch watching movies.
- Work out until you're exhausted.
- Do 15 minutes of yoga or pilates.
- Cancel travel plans. Instead of going somewhere on your vacation days, spend your days at home.
- Cuddle someone for an hour.
- Have sex.
- Lay in a hammock for an hour.
- Get an über instead of driving yourself.
- Order groceries instead of going to the store.
- Find an assistant who can take over some of your admin work.
- And again... take a sabbatical from social media and email.

Anything that makes you feel relaxed, calm, or secure is what we're looking for in the Rest Pennies form. Things that will make you feel, in your body especially, that you have energy. That's what we're after.

PART III

Thought Pennies

I promise I'm not going to spend this entire form ranting about what the internet and social media have done to our brain. But also. I'm not going to NOT talk about it.

If you know anything about nervous system regulation (which, I'm just starting to dive deeper into the actual actions of regulation, although the biological systems stuff is not new to me), you know just how little of our thought is under our control. In fact, there's a colloquial picture that teachers often use to describe just how big our brain would need to be if we were to be conscious of every thought we have and every piece of data... our head would have to be the size of a Volkswagen.

In order to keep us from needing to actively process everything, our subconscious brain does pattern recognition. And that means there are some patterns that are pre-cognitive. Some things we only do because there's hard wiring in there that keeps us from being conscious of them because the brain thinks we don't need the consciousness anymore.

The problem is, those patterns are not serving us.

They're serving someone else's bottom line.

I used to tell a story in one of my productivity workshops about the way the Facebook like button changed from just a "like" option to a range of emotional options. And essentially, the reason was because Facebook studied what made people leave Facebook.

They realized people left because they became aware they were on Facebook. And the "like" button was the thing that made them aware. (Because if I "like" a post that should make me sad, am I saying I'm glad you're sad? Suddenly, I'm thinking, and I'm in my pre-frontal cortex, reasoning, and that's where the control is. The pre-frontal cortex.)

Facebook wanted to keep you out of your pre-frontal cortex, so they made the like button have a range of emotion. To keep you in your brain stem. To keep you in your pre-cognitive state.

To keep you scrolling.

I wouldn't have a problem with this if there was a natural stop to the engagement that social media can provide, but there isn't. The companies don't want there to be a stop. They want your attention as long as you'll give it to them.

But this isn't in your best interest.

When you're so engaged in thinking about things that you saw on Facebook (or ANY social media, news, entertainment site that wants your eyeballs), it can cue you to return for more of the dopamine.

That means, all they have to do is get in front of your eyeballs one time and your control is down for the count.

Unless you have the conscious drive to control your attention.

Most of us are at the mercy of our survival mechanisms, and our unconscious patterns. I just want to see a tiny bit of waking up from that control.

Survival mechanisms, in this case, are the pre-cognitive decision-makers that tell us what decision to make next. In this case, they've been co-opted (for many of us) by a desire to be connected or a desire to know things or a desire to be validated... and that desire is killing our brain.

I know this seems like alarmist talk. But if you could physically see the difference in people when they're in the loop of social media addiction, versus when they're not... if you could see it objectively, you would be as passionate as I am about all of us disciplining ourselves when it comes to our online world.

And I say this as someone who is both quite addicted to social media and also as a person who likes social media. It's where I connect with a lot of my friends. It's also something I regularly detox from.

Specifically because most of us have such a high need for our brains to engage in thinking (deep or shallow thinking), and we're not able to get that part of our brain to work because the back of our brain (or really, the bottom of our brain) is in charge all the time.

But the more those unconscious patterns are in charge, the more our body feels activated.

There's a reason I have to make an entire form of energy production devoted solely to getting our thought processes moving. Because many of us are so caught up in subconscious patterns that are disrupting our ability to think, we are actually shriveling because of it.

I just want to put in a plug for both boredom and also breaks and silence. Even if you don't need the silence for thinking.

Even if you don't have the social media addiction, you might have a work addiction that keeps you from going as deep into your exercise of thought.

And then, of course, there are the people who genuinely don't get fed by thinking, and that will likely mean this form will be a lot of stuff you won't want to do. Or stuff that will drain you. That's okay too. Everyone is different and those differences matter to our decision making.

I'm hopeful to offer some guidelines in this form for how we can engage more deeply with our thoughts.

Thought Penny 1

Dig out an old book you read that made you think
deeply about a topic. Read your favorite parts and
sit with them again.

THIS COULD BE FICTION OR NONFICTION,
because I think deeply about every book I read, no
matter what the subject. But many of us will benefit
the most in the thinking form when we go back
through nonfiction books, looking for old gems.

Too often, those of us who really like consuming
information use nonfiction books as a way to
anesthetize ourselves from having to take action
change things. We head-learn, but we don't heart-learn
or body-learn. So I'm going to add... if you tend to like
thinking and talking more than acting and doing, add

BECCA SYME

an additional level of complexity by asking yourself to take action on something you learn when you do this deep thinking.

I'm especially interested in the action that accompanies the depth of thought. (Action that is produced by depth.)

In general, when we are wired to take action after we understand something (about 25% of the population), the shallow thought encouraged by social media hampers the production of understanding.

So if this resonates with you, I would especially like to see you take regular, intentional breaks from social media.

I know, I promised I wouldn't bring it up. I'm trying.

IF THIS IS A SAVE PENNY:

You will feel energized during or afterward. (For some of us, even the thought of this penny is exciting.

IF THIS IS A DRAIN PENNY:

You'll feel frustrated or feel nothing.

WHERE I SET MINE:

2 cent Save - but it depends on the book. Some books produce more pennies for me because I get so engrossed in them, or they change so much about how I think.

Thought Penny 2

Go looking at the current best-seller lists for nonfiction on Apple, Kobo, or another retailer. Pick one and start today.

MANY OF US DO THIS BY NATURE. WE SEEK OUT new thinking. But I specifically want you to go looking in a place you wouldn't otherwise go. (Like if you're not an Apple user, go check out the Apple bestsellers. Or Kobo.) All of the bestseller lists have the chance to be different. Maybe check out Spotify, Audible, Libsyn, or something that is unfamiliar.

For instance, the Steve Jobs biography is currently on the Kobo best-seller list (and not on the other major lists). And I found a fascinating looking book on the Apple Bestsellers called *How To Know A Person* that I hadn't seen on the other lists.

And on Audible, I picked up *I Know Why The Caged Bird Sings*, Maya Angelou's autobiography, which I've never read.

Sometimes, I'm such a huge fan of the serendipity of what happens to be selling well right now being a guidepost for what I'm going to read next.

Also, if you've never used Kindletrends' tool Kindle Power Search, I would check that out. I know many writers will use it for market research, but I have also been using it to look for books, and find the Top 100s in genres I may not have considered reading before.

Kindletrends is how I found my new love for cozy fantasy, and modified the searches to find the topics of books I wanted. Granted, there aren't those infographics for every genre. But. I'm a big fan.

If we want different results, we have to do different things. So I hope your serendipity-looking goes well.

IF THIS IS A SAVE PENNY:

You will feel excited or stimulated.

IF THIS IS A DRAIN PENNY:

You'll feel frustrated or feel nothing.

WHERE I SET MINE:

5 cent Save

(I know this is a personality trait of mine, but I love searching around and digging around for exactly what I want, so I know this will be more exciting to me than to other people. But I hope you enjoy.)

Thought Penny 3

Ask yourself a random question from a random questions list or from a random question generator. Journal your answer, or talk about it with a friend or loved one.

I'M A HUGE FAN OF LETTING RANDOMNESS into our lives, and getting comfortable with the random. So many of us are striving so much for purpose, we forget that we can't control everything, and introducing randomness is a great way to remind ourselves to be ok with not controlling everything.

So when I selected a random question list, and picked a random number, I got: "What would I do with my life if my opinion was the only one that mattered?"

Oh, Past Becca. I don't know what I was thinking when I put this card in the deck, but it was not, "you're gonna have to perform all these tasks yourself, Becca, so I hope you're ready for the hard truths."

Because there are some hard truths here.

When I ask myself this question, it comes pre-loaded with a bunch of other embedded questions. (Because I know I'm a people pleaser, who started off as a parent pleaser, and I've been doing a lot of work to disentangle that.)

There's a part of me that doesn't know what to do if I'm not looking to someone else to tell me I'm doing it right. (That's the people pleaser part, which is getting developed currently, and is growing up... but the process is painful.) So I have to acknowledge how hard this question will be to answer.

Also, because I'm currently in burnout, and sort of skating along at the bottom of the pit over and over again, the "what choices would I make if only my opinion mattered" are more extreme, because I would cocoon.

Especially while I'm doing all this hard internal work to heal old wounds.

That's not possible if I want to keep living, because living costs money, so I have to consider what I'm willing to sacrifice to keep on living, and what will make the biggest difference in keeping my energy penny production up, long-term.

And this, my friends, is why it's taken me so long to write this book. It's so much more inner work than I considered it would be when I started. My goodness. It's been a lot.

But it's worth it. I know I'm going to live a better life on the other side of this work.

See, not all of this "Thought" form will be deep and intellectual. Some of it will be deep and emotional, too.

Again, though. Worth it.

IF THIS IS A SAVE PENNY:

You will feel excited or stimulated.

IF THIS IS A DRAIN PENNY:

You'll feel frustrated or feel nothing.

WHERE I SET MINE:

10 cent Drain

I'm still glad I did it. But it was quite painful. This is one of those situations, though, where the pain was good. It brought some deeper thinking afterward, which was the whole point.

Thought Penny 4

Make yourself a "thoughtful spot" somewhere in your house. Create a space that facilitates you being quiet and conscious with yourself.

IF YOU SEE THE PHRASE "THOUGHTFUL SPOT" and immediately think of Winnie the Pooh, you are my people. That's exactly what I'm imagining. A restful place that will facilitate your thinking.

This was a little more difficult than I anticipated (the actual making of the spot) because of the way my house is set up, and I don't think I will be alone there.

Every available space was taken up with something, or the spaces that were open were uncomfortable (cold in the winter, downstairs, for instance). So I got a space heater, some blankets and pillows that aren't being used, and now I have a no-tech corner. Now I'm even considering getting one of those bean-bag-chair substitutes.

I have a client whose thoughtful spot used to be in her closet, because it was the only place she knew she could be alone.

Typically, my thoughtful spot is my car. I know I won't look at my phone, I know where to drive where there are no people, and I can turn the music off. Or put on music that supports my thinking.

But I need a place in my house, so I don't use gas driving around when I don't need to.

IF THIS IS A SAVE PENNY:

You will feel excited or stimulated.

IF THIS IS A DRAIN PENNY:

You'll feel frustrated or feel nothing.

WHERE I SET MINE:

(Interestingly, it was a drain when I first wrote the book, because I hadn't created the place yet. But after I created the place, it became a save to go sit down there.)

2 cent Save

Thought Penny 5

When you are overwhelmed, walk away from the computer, the situation, the person, and return later. Take the time in the moment.

YEAH, PAST BECCA DID NOT KID AROUND WHEN it came to the punch pulling. But because this project originally started with a book on overwhelm, I had to at least give a nod to the overwhelm here.

There's so much to unpack here.

There are just so many personality types that experience overwhelm for really good reasons. (I care a lot about how people feel; I care a lot about understanding things; I care a lot about having peace; I care a lot about depth of relationship.) And this isn't even to touch the stuff that happens when our nervous system gets activated.

But when overwhelm is happening for personality reasons, the best thing we can do is do what it's signaling us to do. Walk away. Close the project. Pause the conversation. Wait for the calm to return again. Your brain is telling you a break is required.

Listen to it.

And then give yourself Energy Penny credit for doing it.

After watching *How I Met Your Mother*, I instituted a Pause Function on all my romantic relationships. Whenever we get to a place where emotional intimacy becomes a thing, I explain the Pause Function.

Sometimes, I genuinely need to stop and think. Not from trauma. Just for understanding.

Also, if you're a people pleaser, you might need the Pause Function just to know you're not giving in to someone's will without consciously wanting the thing yourself. It's pretty exhausting to keep watch over, but I think it's beneficial work.

If you're a person who generally doesn't need a Pause Function, I would take this opportunity to think about the people in your life who do need one. Think about what a gift it would be to them if you honored the Pause Function. Let them walk away when they're overwhelmed, and then set the time to come back when they're better.

(Granted, if they're avoidant on too many levels, they may not be healthy enough or invested enough to come back, and then that's a separate conversation. But assuming health and desire for connection, set the time to come back together, after the Pause.)

The way Pause Function works is: When someone says Pause, you both stop, no matter what. And when the person who got Paused gives them time, they get to be the one to ask to Unpause. But the person who Paused has to give them a reasonable assessment for "I'm not ready to unpause yet." And you can ask, "Do you know when you'll be ready?" But the Pauser may not be able to answer that.

Within 24 hours, the conversation needs to get unPaused, unless both parties decide to keep tabling it. But tabling has to be a mutual decision. If only one person is ever in charge of the Pause button, that's unequal.

And if you're the person who's avoiding, because of overwhelm, and you're not currently doing nervous system work or parts work, I need you to do this. It's so important for healthy functioning relationships.

When we're talking about pushing Pause on the manuscript or on a project, or something that requires intellectual (rather than emotional) processing, it's important to still keep the 24 hour rule. Set an intention to come back to the project first thing the next day. Otherwise, the Pause doesn't work to its best effect.

This doesn't mean you're required to make progress the next day. It's just intended to encourage you to not let too long go.

The question we encourage asking on the manuscript front is, "Can I write the next sentence?"

If I can write the next sentence, then I write it. If I can't write the next sentence, I need to think. But there's no reason to force myself to write when I can't. I often need a Pause, and I need to process for a bit.

But again, 24 hours later, I need to ask, "can I write the next sentence."

IF THIS IS A SAVE PENNY:

You will feel excited or stimulated.

IF THIS IS A DRAIN PENNY:

You'll feel frustrated or feel nothing.

WHERE I SET MINE:

5 cent Save

Every time, I think it's going to stress me out to walk away, but it's so much better.

Thought Penny 6

Take a deep dive into a new topic. Find all the resources you can and lose yourself in the pleasure of the new information.

AT ANY ONE POINT IN TIME, I ALWAYS HAVE A topic I'm deep diving on, so I don't as much need the reminder to do this as I need the credit for it.

I'm hopeful that this game will help some of us take credit for the way we deep dive and make pennies for ourselves. Of course, I know this is a source of frustration for some of us, as well, because it's harder to come out of the deep dives.

And to that I say... not everything is about productivity. Some things are about balance, survival, and happiness.

So. Take that for what it's worth.

That's also why I encourage only playing each card once per day. If I've done a deep dive for the day (like I'm about to work through the next lesson in this Nervous System Activation course), then that's the last thing I'll do on that topic for the day.

I know I'm going to want to go back, because if I had my druthers, I would just keep deep diving until I was done (which might be months from now). But I have other things to do. Like finish this book. So I need to get through other cards besides this one.

Still. When this provides me as many pennies as it does, I don't want to ignore it for too long. I might not intentionally play this card every day, for the 25 cents (or 50 cents, depending on where I land) it's going to provide me.

But I can't ignore this card for very long. It's one of my biggest sources of energy production, which means if I don't fulfill this need, it will become an equal energy drain.

IF THIS IS A SAVE PENNY:

You will feel excited or stimulated.

IF THIS IS A DRAIN PENNY:

You'll feel frustrated or feel nothing.

WHERE I SET MINE:

25 cent Save

Thought Penny 7

Create space in your day for thinking. Don't wait for later, Macy. However you think the best, take fifteen to twenty minutes (longer if you have the time).

THIS IS WELL-TROD SPACE FOR ME. IF YOU know me at all, you know I'm constantly reminding people who need thinking time to take it.

So I won't say much more here, except for one thing.

Even if you don't intentionally think about the thing you want to think about, still take the time. Even if your thoughts wander. Even if you just give yourself the time away from everything to let those thoughts have a second.

I usually use some kind of a prompt to keep my thoughts refocusing. I'll either have a journal in front of me and write things down, or I'll turn on Otter and let myself think aloud or I'll type something on a phone screen (or find a meme that reminds me of the thing I need to think about) just to remind myself.

Don't expect your brain to do all the work for you. Sometimes you have to help your brain think about the things you want to think about. And if there are other things on the train tracks that need to get thought of first, then think of those things and get them out of the way so you can have the tracks back.

Mental discipline isn't easy for many of us, and it triggers some of us into thought spirals. (Again, practice the body work to regulate the nervous system.)

But think of mental discipline like moving the Mississippi River. Sometimes, the thoughts will flow back their old way, and that's not a bad thing. We keep digging the trench over time, and it will help the river to move. (As long as we're not attacking it, and are instead being gracious with it.)

Ok, I'll stop. But. Consider it.

If this is a Save Penny:

You will feel excited or stimulated.

· · ·

IF THIS IS A DRAIN PENNY:

You'll feel frustrated or feel nothing.

WHERE I SET MINE:

1 cent Save

Thought Penny 8

Sit with one of the bigger philosophical questions of our time. Don't expect an outcome, just let yourself think deeply about it.

YOU MIGHT RESIST THIS, AND IF YOU DO, PUT it as a Drain, and then use the card gently. This may not be something you do when you're in an otherwise "below the line" emotional state.

But if this will make energy pennies for you, I want to make sure you at least consider it.

For some of us, this will be a Leak, because we can't come to resolution. So don't do this card if it will be a Leak for you.

I typically do this when I know I'm going to spend time with a friend who's very philosophical. I have a friend here who is very intellectual, and every time we meet, I come prepared with philosophy or theology to discuss. It's always fun. But I have to think about it first, so I acknowledge that I need time on my own to prepare.

For me, this often involves reading, but it doesn't take much reading to set me off into thinking.

Again, if that's not for you, because your deep-in-thought space doesn't bring you Energy Pennies, I would consider either changing this card or ignoring it.

Totally up to what you feel is best for yourself.

IF THIS IS A SAVE PENNY:

You will feel excited or stimulated.

IF THIS IS A DRAIN PENNY:

You'll feel frustrated or feel nothing.

WHERE I SET MINE:

1 cent Save

Thought Penny 9

What is coming for you in the next days, weeks, or months? Look at your calendar and think through what will happen.

SOME OF US WILL ABSOLUTELY THRIVE IN THIS place. We'll get so many energy pennies from thinking about the future, planning. If that's you, make sure you do this often.

But some of us are already filled with dread at the thought of having to do this. If that's you, skip this card or change it.

Not everyone is helped by thinking about the future. In fact, for some of us, this card will be a Leak. (When we're forced to do it, we can't bring ourselves back into the present moment to take action, so the future is just a generally scary place to hang out.)

If you're someone who is inspired by the future, this card has two purposes.

First are the pennies we get from the thinking and dreaming. When you're picturing the great things that could happen, and you're wired this way, you'll get pennies from it. Important pennies.

Second are the pennies from taking today's step. It's so important not to disconnect these from each other. The purpose of looking at the future is to take steps to create it. So if we're going to do step one, we need to do step two.

Around the BFA (my coaching business), we call this OTT. One Thing Today. And if you get pennies from the future, the growth edge is to make sure we're always doing something to make that future real for everyone else.

If I see a future where I am connected to a person, I take a step today to make that happen.

If I see a future where I am healthier, I take literal steps to make that happen.

If I see a future where I've finished a book, I open the manuscript and ask, "can I write the next sentence?"

That's the way to bring the future forward. Progress.

IF THIS IS A SAVE PENNY:

You will feel excited or stimulated.

. . .

IF THIS IS A DRAIN PENNY:

You'll feel frustrated, spiral out, or feel nothing.

WHERE I SET MINE:

2 cent Save

Thought Penny 10

Phone a friend who likes to think deeply about things and ask them for their opinion on a current difficulty or question you are facing.

MANY OF US WHO SPEND TIME IN OUR BRAINS (thinking a lot) struggle more to reach out than others. So this might be a task that takes some energy for us. But hopefully it will also produce some.

And again, just a reminder, if this is too much of a Drain for you, or it's not resonating, change the card to something else that has to do with thinking. (I'll give some suggestions later in these chapters.)

You can approach this conversation philosophically (where you're asking for a hypothetical opinion) or you can talk about a real situation. But the goal is to let them process it and think about it, and then come back to you.

I have some very deep friends, and what I find I enjoy the most about them is the fact that they will keep talking to me about a situation long after I've opened the conversation. They'll continue to send me memes over time, or they'll continue to ask questions at a later date.

If you have these kinds of friends, cherish them. They can often provide perspective you'd never consider, especially the longer you give them to think about it. (The less pressure you put on them during the conversation to have answers.)

Gold, I tell you.

IF THIS IS A SAVE PENNY:

You will feel comforted or connected.

IF THIS IS A DRAIN PENNY:

You'll feel frustrated or disconnected.

WHERE I SET MINE:

2 cent Save

Thought Penny 11

Find a documentary you haven't watched before and turn it on. Sit with a notebook and jot notes about what you're learning.

MANY OF US DO NOT NEED ENCOURAGEMENT to do this. And you may already be doing it, in which case, give yourself credit for it.

Because I coach a lot of writers, I see a lot that they'll get stuck and looking for ideas, and at the same time, they're reluctant to do something like this because it seems like a waste of time.

But the way many of our brains are wired, we need the additional information to spark new ideas. Even though we might also enjoy watching the documentary, we still need the stimulation.

It's what makes words happen.

Even if you're not a writer, though, this can still be an activity that brings you pennies. And depending on how many you need for the day, this might be enough.

I do think the "notebook" or "notes" part is important as well. What I don't want this card to turn into is an excuse to scroll on our phones. Be attentive to the learning and if the learning gets boring, turn it off and find a new one.

Too many of us use learning opportunities as background noise for scrolling on our phones, and then we wonder why we're not feeling the benefits of the learning. But unless you're doing something like playing a game to distract part of your brain so you can concentrate on the doc, the phone is not helping.

The goal of this exercise is new thoughts. Progress. That's a theme in so many of the "Thought" cards. We think to get farther or deeper. We think to become more certain. We think to make progress.

Hopefully this will help you.

IF THIS IS A SAVE PENNY:

You will feel interested and stimulated.

IF THIS IS A DRAIN PENNY:

You'll feel frustrated or bored.

WHERE I SET MINE:

1 cent Save

Thought Penny 12

Make a spreadsheet of data for a problem you're facing or a decision you need to make. Gather all the data you can. What does it tell you?

NOT EVERY DECISION INCLUDES DATA YOU CAN put into a spreadsheet, of course. Although you'd be surprised what you can use spreadsheets for... when I was applying to grad school, I created a ranking system to help me choose which programs to say yes to first. That spreadsheet was a thing of beauty.

There are very few things I can't quantify in a numerical ranking system and make a spreadsheet out of. I even wrote a course in our Author4Life library called "Marketing For Introverts" where I use a system of rankings to help determine what marketing you should and shouldn't do as an author. (Or how to prioritize.)

When this is a drain for you, I actively (and sometimes aggressively) encourage you to ignore spreadsheets. Even when it feels like everyone is pressuring you to use them. Sometimes numbers only overwhelm.

(Although, again, I also use spreadsheets for words. I do a lot of my plotting in spreadsheet forms, as well.)

But because many of us are spreadsheet fans, I wanted to remind us that seeing data laid out is often a signal for those of us who need to look objectively at it. We need to see it in front of us. This serves as a reminder that when you need to do that, and it generates pennies for you, give yourself credit for it.

IF THIS IS A SAVE PENNY:

You will feel interested and stimulated.

IF THIS IS A DRAIN PENNY:

You'll feel frustrated or bored.

WHERE I SET MINE:

1 cent Save

Optional Additional Thought Pennies

I HAVE BEEN COLLECTING SOME ACTIVITIES that I think you might want to consider adding to your thought pennies list, but which I did not include on the printed cards. So here are some thoughts for where you could add other cards to your own deck.

- Go to a museum.
- Take a class or workshop.
- Join a philosophy or theology discussion group.
- Watch avant garde films.
- Read an old philosophy or theology book. (Specifically, something written before 1900.)
- Go for a walk with no music and no podcast and no speaking to someone on the phone.
- Lie on the floor in the middle of the room and stare at the ceiling.
- Spend an entire day without screens. (I wish more of us would do this one, and I almost put this one in the deck, but I didn't want to trigger

anyone, because dopamine addiction is a real thing.)

- Find someone with a different viewpoint from yours on an important topic and listen to understand. Listen for empathy and understanding.
- Buy one of the BestSelf Decks or a deck like Philosophical Questions for Curious Minds and work through those cards. (The BestSelf Decks, by the way, are the best decks on the market except for the one done by Tonight's Conversation. I did some pretty extensive research on decks to make sure nothing existed like what I wanted to bring to the market, and I found some of them to be so incredibly helpful. The BestSelf decks were some of the absolute best. But let me tell you, if you ever want to get into some deep discussions, get the Tonight's Conversation decks, especially the Relationship Debates deck. You will have some wild conversations.)

Anything that makes you feel competent or deep or more certain is what we're looking for in the Thought Pennies form. Things that will produce deep conversations, more knowledge, and more clarity. That's what we're after.

PART IV
Spirit Pennies

When I was dividing up the types of energy pennies we could make, I wanted one specifically for "connection" (both with myself and with others), and it just didn't feel like it had the same quality as Joy.

We may feel happiness, when we feel connection (like I'm encouraging in the "spirit" form). The deeper the connection, the more likely it will induce us to move from happiness into hopefulness and into security, so we can feel more true joy. More "nothing is required of you" feelings.

A deep connection to other people, to the world, to the divine (if that's something you want to connect with), and to yourself.

Spirit wholeness. That's what this form is after.

Spirit Penny 1

Call the person you feel the safest with and ask them if they can video chat or meet for lunch. This week.

I KNOW "SAFE" MIGHT BE A WEIRD WORD. FOR you, it might be "favorite" or "best friend" or "spouse/partner." But whoever is your closest, most integrated friend (a person who wants the best for you), that's the person I want you to spend time with.

This might create a drain on some of us, because we don't have this person in our lives right now, and I want to acknowledge the pain of that state of being. We might have lost that person, we might not ever have had them, and I don't want to downplay that place.

It's awful.

My hope is, there's someone in your life that could be an emotional stand-in for that person (even if it's your therapist or spiritual director). I'd rather see you spend time with someone who fills you up and who you can fill up, but also, when you pay for someone to allow you vulnerability, you don't have to take on their burdens in return. Upside?

I pay a therapist to allow me complete vulnerability.

But my spirit feels significantly better after my therapy appointments (which I had every week, when I was in burnout). I could feel the difference in my spirit because of it.

If this person is a friend/partner, and you need them to fill your spirit pennies, you may have to say ahead of time, "I'll fill yours and you fill mine" so you get equal time being filled. However you make this happen, I want to see you connect with someone who makes you feel at home.

IF THIS IS A SAVE PENNY:

You will feel heart-warm during and afterward.

IF THIS IS A DRAIN PENNY:

You'll feel frustrated or feel nothing. (This might be temporary, also, so I want to encourage you to re-place this one in a few months, just in case it's changed.)

. . .

Where I set mine:

50 cent Save

Spirit Penny 2

Go for a nature walk and let yourself soak in all
the aliveness around you.

BECAUSE THIS IS A SPIRIT PENNY, WE WANT TO
approach this with a sense of connection to the natural
world. Not just observing the beauty or being a passive
member of the encounter with nature. But physically
aware of the connection we have to the natural world.

I will often intentionally touch natural things when I do
this more "connection-driven" walking. Like put my
hand on a tree trunk. Or take off my shoes and put my
toes in the grass/water. Or pick a flower and put my
face in it. (I especially love to do this with lilacs in
June.)

I'm not as worried about the physical exercise—one of
my "Spirit Penny" moments recently was driving

around in a cart in an open-air national park setting. I wasn't necessarily touching everything all the time. But every time I could, I would try to connect with the nature around me.

IF THIS IS A SAVE PENNY:

You will feel heart-warm during and afterward.

IF THIS IS A DRAIN PENNY:

You'll feel frustrated or feel nothing. (This might be temporary or seasonal, so I want to encourage you to re-try this one in a few months, just in case it's changed.)

WHERE I SET MINE:

25 cent Save

Spirit Penny 3

Pray.

Or meditate.

Or both.

THIS IS NOT ABOUT RELIGION FOR ME. Specifically, this is about connection to my spirit or to the Spirit. Something other than the biological fear response soup going on in our brains.

I'm looking for beneficial connection to something that has the capacity to cut through that fear.

Some of you need the reminder that you do connect to the Universe or to God. Some of you need the reminder to connect with your self.

That's what I want you to do.

For me and for my personality, this is one of the most important card practices I ever do. I have a deep need for connection, and I know the outside world cannot provide enough for me.

Even with the most beneficial of friendships, I know I will still be wanting more than I ever get. And that's not a fair thing to put on the people in my life.

They can't meet this need for me. But I can meet it for myself. I can get glimmers of it from them, but I can't get the real, mainline spirit pennies from anything other than God.

When I meditate, because I'm not a "clear your mind" meditator, I tend to meditate ON things, rather than try to clear my mind to mediate. I've just learned, that's not my personality, so I try to focus my thoughts instead of empty them.

(You're welcome to try to empty thoughts if you want to. I don't think there's anything wrong with it. Just that it doesn't work for me.)

But when I meditate on, I pick something really beautiful, poetic, deep, or connecting to meditate on.

I pick a lot of poetry (Rumi, David Whyte, Maya Angelou) and I will occasionally pick philosophy or theology or sacred texts. I'm not always looking for comfort, either. Sometimes, I'm looking for expansion.

So I might read someone who expands my horizons, rather than someone I know I already like.

I do pray, and I specifically pray to God, but I don't pray the way I think most of you were taught in Sunday School to pray. I pray with my imagination. It's a practice I've had for many years, but it also helps me stay connected in my spirit. The primary focus is in imagining your picture of God and diving deep into all the elements of that picture and how it informs your life.

However you pray or meditate, I encourage you to try doing it regularly. You could do mind-clearing work. You could do repetitive prayers. Whatever works the best for you.

I just want to see us be more connected, in all directions.

IF THIS IS A SAVE PENNY:

You will feel heart-warm during and afterward.

IF THIS IS A DRAIN PENNY:

I want to acknowledge that many of us have religious trauma that has impacted us for many years, and even the mention of God is likely to bring that up. You have my heart, and if I could take that trauma away, I would. Please ignore me if the pain is too great. I would sit in the pain with you and heal it if I could. But I can't. So I will just say, you have all my love, and all my deepest sorrow. That kind of wound knows no bounds.

WHERE I SET MINE:

2 cent Save

Spirit Penny 4

Write out all the positive emotions you're feeling. Start with happy, then grateful, then hopeful, then secure.

THIS IS SPECIFICALLY A "CONNECTION WITH self" card, and this one is pretty important to me. If you've ever seen Laurel Mellin's work on emotional resilience, you'll be familiar with the "cycle" tool.

I use the cycle tool regularly (and was using it daily for a long segment of my life). It helps me feel more connected to myself when I'm allowed to feel emotions safely.

And I want to also add, this might not be something you're comfortable doing, and that's also okay. Some of us genuinely don't connect with our positive emotions, and trying to do that stresses us out. You're welcome to replace this with any "connection to self" activity you'd like.

I would replace this card with doing nervous system work instead. Do "connection to self" work rather than "connection to emotions" work. We may talk about some nervous system work later, but I'm going to recommend Episode 324 of the Mark Groves podcast (with Sarah Baldwin) again… she's the person whose regulation work has resonated the most with me.

Or just put a "drain" on this card and leave it be. Totally up to you.

If you're a person who needs more internal connection to your emotions, I'll recommend Mellin's work. I've really appreciated it.

IF THIS IS A SAVE PENNY:

You will feel heart-warm during and afterward.

IF THIS IS A DRAIN PENNY:

You'll feel frustrated or feel nothing.

WHERE I SET MINE:

1 cent Save

I do this regularly throughout the day, but if I'm playing the game, I only count the card once.

Spirit Penny 5

Tell someone how much you love them and specifically what you love about them.

BECAUSE THIS IS THE "CONNECTION" FORM, I'm going to remind everyone that the goal of these cards is to **make** pennies for us. So if this declaration will cause conflict (like you're reaching out to someone that you have a rupture with), don't reach out to that person. This is not a "healing" experience for someone else.

This is meant to produce connection in you. Spirit pennies have a wholeness to them. So pick a person who has a good connection with you and tell them how much you love them.

I'm doing the cards along with you, so here's what this looks like.

I reached out to my mother to talk about summer plans, and she made a comment about something she'd been doing and I noticed it was a different pattern from what she'd done in the past.

I stopped the conversation and told her how much I loved her, and how much I loved that she was always trying to work on herself, and what an inspiration it was to keep working on myself.

It's important that we are specific, and that the utterance is genuine (to actually grow the relationship). But I encourage you to do this today.

IF THIS IS A SAVE PENNY:

You will feel heart-warm during and afterward.

IF THIS IS A DRAIN PENNY:

You'll feel frustrated or feel nothing.

WHERE I SET MINE:

2 cent Save

When I went back through to edit this book, I was doing some of the cards again, for the sake of seeing if we were still in the same place, and I had an interesting thought that I posted on my Facebook page. I'm going to include it here, because I do think this reflection on the practice of vulnerability is important.

I've been editing the Energy book and am re-doing the practice of some of the exercises, and yesterday, I came across the "tell someone what you love about them" card.

I had a friend over yesterday who is quite empathetic, and just her presence in my house was like a balm, and I found myself telling her what a gift her inner empath can be, as a way of trying to express gratitude for something I'd really needed. But I said, "Empathy is such a gift" instead of "you are such a gift," and as I'm reflecting on the Energy Pennies work this morning, that gave me pause.

The vulnerability of saying, "you are a gift to me," struck me.

It shouldn't be a surprise to anyone that I think this deeply about things, but I've been ruminating on this now for most of yesterday and now again this morning as I pick the editing back up again.

It is extremely vulnerable to say, "I love you," to someone. Or to say, "you are a gift to me," to someone. And I find it very easy for me to call out the names of talents in the people I love, and talk about how amazing their actions and presence are as a gift to the world.

But wow, saying, "I love you and you are a gift to me"... that's a scary thing.

I know I could say it to my sister or my mother at any time, and there's no danger there. But even other members of my family, there's some kind of "uh-oh" there. And certainly, to all my friends (only because we haven't known each other as long as I've known my mother and sister).

Yet, when I gave the suggestion originally in the EP book, I know I did the practice--I did every penny when I wrote it--so I know I actually did this, but it does make me wonder if I took the safe route and said it to my mom or sister.

Anyway, I saw a video from one of the people I regularly follow yesterday that said, "when you feel like withdrawing, that's the time for 'I love you' and when you feel like pulling away, that's the time for connection." It was a reminder that in an equal relationship, withdrawing affection or connection or love isn't helping the relationship. It's only protecting you.

I've spent a lot of years protecting myself from rejection and abandonment. And I've spent a lot of years withdrawing as a way of not getting hurt.

But that's not the goal of the practice. The goal of the practice (especially of this particular card) is the growth of connection. That requires vulnerability, which means, you can hurt me. If I love you, and I am vulnerable with you, that means you can hurt me. And for many of us, that's too dangerous a place to go.

So I'm not telling you to do anything different than you're doing. Or encouraging anyone to do what I do. Just reflecting for thought.

I'm going to practice the card today. And as I dive back into the editing, I'm a little scared for how the book is going to keep hurting my feelings. But... I'll get through it.

Spirit Penny 6

Go to a botanical garden or butterfly sanctuary or somewhere that's teeming with life. Spend an hour there, just existing.

I RECENTLY WENT TO HONOLULU FOR THE first time and visited a place called Waimea Falls. It was a 5K walk through this lush, vibrant park, and ended in the view of these gorgeous falls. There were hundreds of types of trees, plants, and flowers, each one labeled.

I haven't felt so peaceful in a long time as I felt inside that place. Even just sitting down in the middle of the trek and staring at all the green around me was a balm.

Of course, it's winter in Minnesota right now, but I found a greenhouse I can visit that will get me in touch with some natural elements (and I have plants inside my house now, for this very reason). There's just something about live plants or living animals that speaks to the natural part of our soul.

If you can be intentional about this, in whatever season you're able, please do this. And I don't mean a park local to you, if you're able to. I would get out of your comfort zone. The feeling I'm going for here is the "surrounded" feeling.

IF THIS IS A SAVE PENNY:

You will feel heart-warm during and afterward.

IF THIS IS A DRAIN PENNY:

You'll feel frustrated or feel nothing.

WHERE I SET MINE:

5 cent save

Spirit Penny 7

Go to a vibrant and beautiful public place with a crowd of people and sit in the midst of that crowd.

OK, TO THE MISANTHROPES IN THE CROWD, because I know there are some reading this: it's ok if this is a drain penny for you. If at all possible, I'd love to see you still do the card, just to see if your attitude changes at all. And if it doesn't, it's a drain, and that's that.

But here's what I'd like this action to look like.

Specifically pick somewhere that is both beautiful and crowded. For me, there's a segment of the Mall of America (which is in my hometown) where the hanging lights are so beautiful, and there's a Caribou Coffee, and you can sit in the lights and brightness and stare at the crowds of people, but still be in a pretty quiet and secluded area with a lot of beauty around.

Any individual mall might not be this way for you, so it doesn't have to be a mall. But anywhere that's both beautiful and public.

Sitting in the midst of the crowd is the main goal, just to be around the vibrancy of people. But then I have an additional challenge.

Think well of each person you see.

Even just a wishing well. If you are a praying person, pray for them. Compliment them in your head. Think something nice about them.

And if that's too far for you, then stop at the crowd part. But just see what happens if you change the lens. Many of you won't do this, just because it seems so weird. But it's become one of my favorite things to do. In fact, I love living so near the MOA for this exact reason and those of you who've come to our in-person conference (which we host at the MOA) might even have been to this place on the third floor. It's nothing special in the grand scheme, but it puts me in a place that I think is pretty, and a place where I can have my back to the wall, and where I can wish well of people.

And again, it's ok if this is a drain for you, or a nope-out. Not everyone likes crowded places to begin with, and some of us have chronic illnesses (or illnesses or disabilities) that prevent us from spending time in public. This would be too much of a drain to be worth keeping in your deck if those things are true. Modify things to fit in your life.

That's why the deck is customizable. Question my premise, when it doesn't fit with your life.

IF THIS IS A SAVE PENNY:

You will feel heart-warm during and afterward.

IF THIS IS A DRAIN PENNY:

Even the thought of doing this might be frustrating. And when you do it, you might get overwhelmed. It may also spark no joy in you at all, and that would be at least a small drain.

WHERE I SET MINE:

5 cent save

Spirit Penny 8

Hug an animal (a willing animal) if you have one in your home. Or go to a shelter and offer to pet or walk the animals there.

(Not a buffalo in Yellowstone... my editor added... lol)

One of my friends can't have cats in her apartment complex, but she has always been a cat person. So she takes her daughter, every week, to the animal shelter to sit with the cats.

And they **sit** with the cats. Sometimes, they play, but generally speaking, they're trying to help socialize the cats, so they want to really hold them. They spend hours, sometimes, just petting the animals and playing with them.

She made a comment on one of her IG photos once about how peaceful it is holding those cats, even when they aren't hers, and it reminded me of just how much most of us need physical touch and aren't getting it. Especially after the pandemic.

So I'm going to issue you a challenge.

If you don't have animals in your home, go find some to sit with (legally and willingly) and hold. Put them on your body if you can (where they're sitting on you) or hold them.

Heartbeat to heartbeat is what I'm looking for.

I had an amazing cat for fifteen years, and he used to come onto my bed when I was reading and just sit on my heart. I don't know if he knew what he was doing, but just the presence of his heartbeat on mine (or when he would sit on my neck) was so centering.

And if this is making you feel sad, just reading this, because you can't have animals or don't have them in your house, close your eyes and feel me hugging you. Also. Go find a place to hug animals, walk them, or pet them. Spend time with heartbeats.

This can also be other people, but I do think there's something different about animals because they love unconditionally. I think that's why we all like having pets (or those of us who do have pets love pets). They are little unconditional lovers.

Ok, some of them are big unconditional lovers (don't think I didn't consider getting a mastiff once, only to realize they weigh more than my adult human sister).

Right now, this is a drain card for me because I haven't had a pet since Mikhail (the cat I mentioned above), and I'm still a little raw from having him gone. But I know I'll get there, where I can go to the shelter again. Or pet someone else's animal.

I also had a friend recommend weighted heartbeat stuffed animals, if you are quite allergic or if you live somewhere that pets aren't allowed. I haven't tried them yet, so I can't speak to it, but just knowing how much the little heartbeat mattered to me, I do think I should at least try.

IF THIS IS A SAVE PENNY:

You will feel heart-warm during and afterward. Centered. Comforted. Restored.

IF THIS IS A DRAIN PENNY:

You'll feel frustrated or feel nothing.

WHERE I SET MINE:

1 cent Drain

Only because of the grief, and I still feel a lot of grief about him being gone. But I will get there. :)

Spirit Penny 9

Sit in a quiet room, with nothing on and no screens around you, and feel the peace of the quiet.

THIS WILL BE A STRAIN FOR SOME OF US WHO do everything we can to avoid being alone and quiet.

Hopefully you have some emotional regulation skills at the ready, because I want you to sit somewhere with no tech and no screens.

You can let your mind wander, or you can try to direct your thoughts. But just let the silence be around you.

I know some of us have trauma around silence, and it might not be for us. I always encourage experimentation when something resonates, but don't push yourself if you get extremely uncomfortable during silence. This can be a card you skip.

If this is a Save Penny:

You will feel heart-warm during and afterward.

If this is a Drain Penny:

You'll feel scared or frustrated before, and after, you might be actively angry at me for suggesting it (in which case, I am genuinely sorry for this and I understand... some of us are not built for silence). Hopefully you'll know that before you do it, and save yourself from that.

Where I set mine:

1 cent Save

Spirit Penny 10

Read a David Whyte poem. Or Maya Angelou. Or Joy Harjo. Read every word aloud.

I'M A HUGE FAN OF POETRY TO MAKE US FEEL more connected to humanity or to ourselves, and specifically spoken aloud poetry. Poetry you have to sit with and listen to. I'm going to make some suggestions, because I have favorites.

If you like to listen to poetry read aloud, I highly recommend listening to David Whyte read "Everything Is Waiting For You" on YouTube. It's a beautiful poem, and he's so lyrical when he reads aloud.

He has some recordings of reading his poetry alive that one of my friends owned, and I've never been able to get my hands on them. But they were fantastic. I love listening to poetry aloud.

One of my favorites (for both reading aloud and for meditation, because... it's a deep one) is "Wonder" by Maya Angelou. In general, I find poetry to be much deeper than just the words, and this is one that I sit with often.

And in general, I love Joy Harjo, but my favorite to read aloud is "Call It Fear" and in those moments when I just need "any other voice to stay alive with," I think of her. You'll see what I mean when you read the poem.

Another favorite, Gerard Manley Hopkins (who might be too religious for some of us), has an incredibly complex linguistic methodology. He reminds me of an Alanis Morrissette song sometimes (who is another amazing and lyrical poet). But I really love the depth of thought there.

Or Rumi. Or Emily Dickenson. Or really anyone who will put complicated, interesting phrases and thoughts together that I can read aloud and challenge myself with. Feeling a deep connection to the world and to humanity often comes with exposure.

I hope you get some exposure to connection today.

IF THIS IS A SAVE PENNY:

You will feel heart-warm and inspired.

. . .

IF THIS IS A DRAIN PENNY:

You'll feel bored or intimidated, and it won't get better as you move through the poems.

WHERE I SET MINE:

2 cent Save

Spirit Penny 11

Listen to music without doing something else at
the same time. Just lay there and soak in the
music.

LATELY, I'VE BEEN LISTENING TO WHOLE
albums. Lying on the ground in my living room. Instead
of scrolling social media to distract myself, I'm
listening to entire albums and paying attention to the
music. Listening to the words. Repeating the words out
loud sometimes.

My next goal will be to get a vinyl record player and
start listening to the vinyls I still have. And maybe buy
more vinyls.

There's something about the consumption of entire
albums that still really soothes me. I love the musical
journey and the poetry of the lyrics (some of the music

you would scoff at has some of the most poetic lyrics ever—especially if you take the context into consideration or the expression into consideration). We rush to judge quickly and don't rush to empathy fast enough.

Anyway.

Listen to a whole album for me. I'm going to do Alanis today. One of her later albums fewer people listen to. I may not be able to lie on the floor the whole time because this book is calling me. But I still want the energy pennies...

IF THIS IS A SAVE PENNY:

You will feel engaged during and afterward. Even if your mind wanders a bit. Or a lot.

IF THIS IS A DRAIN PENNY:

You'll feel disengaged or frustrated and won't want to do it.

WHERE I SET MINE:

1 cent Save

Spirit Penny 12

Sing.

Not to sound beautiful.

To make your breath alive.

IF YOU EVER TALK TO PROFESSIONAL SINGERS (or even amateur singers who still regularly sing), you'll hear a fullness to their voices when they talk because they've had to practice breathing most of their lives.

In fact, I'd wager to bet, you won't find people more in control of their breath than professional singers. When you learn to sing, you have to learn to breathe.

So when you do this card, when you sing, I want you to focus on breathing. Take deep breaths, even if you have to miss singing lyrics. And push with your diaphragm (that little muscle below your lungs that helps push your breath).

Try it physically with your hand once. Rest your hand flat on your upper stomach, start singing something, and then push on your stomach like you'd pat yourself if you were telling someone you were full.

Feel the rush of air that rounds out your tone? That's what singers are aiming to do with their breath. Have better control over their tone.

But beyond that, breathing is one of the best tactics for nervous system regulation there is. Singing engages deep breathing, and free, deep breathing is one of the ways your body uses to remind yourself that you're safe.

When I feel dysregulated, I get in the car and sing. There's nothing quite like Amy Lee to get your deep breath engaged. In fact, there's a segment at the end of the bridge on "Everybody's Fool" that tests my breath control every time. I'll sometimes just play that minute or so of the song over and over to work out my breathing.

I can almost feel the rush of relief to my body just thinking about it, because I already did this card today. And because I love singing but live in a house where I can't sing whenever and however I want, this card is worth more pennies to me than it might be to others.

But even if you aren't a singer, still sing. The goal isn't

to make other people think you've got a pretty voice. The goal is to engage your breathing more deeply.

And yes, we could say, "breathe deeply" but it really does make a difference to put the breath to music.

If you don't want people hearing you, sing in the car. But sing.

IF THIS IS A SAVE PENNY:

You will feel alive and energized.

IF THIS IS A DRAIN PENNY:

You'll feel disengaged or frustrated and won't want to do it.

WHERE I SET MINE:

10 cent Save

Optional Additional Spirit Pennies

I HAVE BEEN COLLECTING SOME ACTIVITIES that I think you might want to consider adding to your spirit pennies list, but which I did not include on the printed cards. So here are some thoughts for where you could add other cards to your own deck.

- Get into water (bath, pool, ocean, etc.—showers don't count for the purposes of this action)
- Go to a cathedral, mosque, sacred wood, or other sacred space where you feel connected.
- Have sex (this is the "make love" kind of sex) with a connected partner.
- Have an open and honest conversation (staying connected with yourself and your conversation partner) with someone who will hold space for your grief, pain, loneliness.
- Listen to Sarah Baldwin talk about the nervous system and how so much of the fear and pain

we feel can be healed by regulating our nervous systems. (I'm a fan of Episode 324 of the Mark Groves Podcast.)

- Go to a masseuse who specializes in healing massage or in reiki.
- Spend a day at the spa, and have every area of your body tended to.
- Practice daily gratitude.

Anything that makes you feel connected and whole is what we're looking for in the Spirit Pennies form. Things that will produce deep connection to yourself, to the world, to God, to the universe, to humanity. That's what we're after.

PART V
Joy Pennies

The study of joy has risen in cultural discussion lately, which is appropriate. After we've been through a massive disconnecting event like the Covid-19 pandemic, among many other disconnecting events of the last couple of decades, it was time for the pendulum to swing back.

I want to be very intentional about the way I'm using the word "Joy" in this book. When I say "Joy," I do not mean "elated" or "happy" only. I might be "happy" doing things that hurt me, and I might be "happy" disconnecting or checking out. (Or I might think that makes me happy.)

But what I mean by "Joy" is "completely secure." Joy that makes me feel peace or security or connection. It's a state of being where nothing else is required of me.

I am good as I am. The world is good as it is. Nothing is required of me in this moment.

The peace that passes understanding is a peace that does not require understanding. It just is. Security.

With happiness, I have to continue to produce the feeling (continue to stimulate the neurons producing the happy chemicals) in order to maintain the feeling. Like sugar or an orgasm. But Joy is a secure feeling that does not require stimulation.

That's the word for Joy. It is enough. In a secure way. Not a tired way. Not "I've had enough." But "I am enough."

Again, I reference the work of Laurel Mellin, where the goal of the positive emotion cycle is to land in the secure feeling. It does start with happiness, but then you feel each positive emotion in consequence, and the end of that cycle is a feeling of "this is enough, I am enough," etc.

Let me make a quick observation here. Given the colloquial discussions about "joy" everywhere, I want to be really careful to differentiate between things that numb our pain (things that appear to make us happy in the moment, but which are only a distraction from the fact that overall, we're terrified) and things that actually produce peace. When you do something that makes you feel truly joyful (not just a fleeting moment of happiness), it should produce a security in you that will have hopefulness, gratitude, and happiness all rolled up into one ball. (Again, the progress through the emotion cycle.)[1]

So as much as I'm a "let's make joy pennies" person in the colloquial way, where we're mostly focused on happiness, I am much more of a "let's make a life that doesn't terrify us" person, which might seem like an artificial distinction for some of us. But.

I had to say it.

The way I hear most people in the productivity industrial complex talking about joy as a way to increase productivity actually worries me. It feels like an anesthetic for the actual problem.

I want us to fix the actual problem.

And I want us to stop anesthetizing ourselves to a life that has no joy embedded in it, where we are primarily being consumed for our resources, and no one is caring for our souls.

What I'm looking for in these cards is a hit of happiness that can push us through the positive emotion cycle, all the way to that secure feeling. Happiness that reminds you, you're ok and nothing more is required of you.

That's a tall order, and some of us need some inner work first, before we can get there. I realize that. I think I just want all of us to get there. I can see a future where we're all healed from those fear wounds, and it's really beautiful. But taking a bubble bath isn't going to produce enough joy to heal my inner wounds.

I have to actually heal those wounds myself.

Super happy intro to the joy chapter, eh? Phew, Becca.

The base cards for Joy Pennies are listed in the next chapters. At the end of the current cards, I will make a list of other possible Joy Pennies cards that you could make.

And if you ever find yourself doing something and you want to remind yourself that you've made Joy Pennies, share it on the hashtag #joypennies on social media. I'd love to see it.

And now. To the pennies themselves.

Joy Penny 1

Get out into nature and put your toes into the grass. Stay there for five minutes, just feeling life around you.

WHEN I ENCOURAGE PEOPLE GOING OUTSIDE, I don't just mean stand at the window and look out. I legitimately mean to get out into the external world.

If there is grass, stand in the grass. If there is sand, stand in the sand. (No concrete, no sidewalks. This is a nature card.) If you would rather stand on your deck and look out at nature, rather than be in it, I'm good there.

IF THIS IS A SAVE PENNY:

You will feel refreshed afterward.

IF THIS IS A DRAIN PENNY:

You'll dread doing it and you won't feel good afterward.

WHERE I SET MINE:

5 cent Save

Joy Penny 2

Watch an episode of your favorite TV show or throw in your favorite movie.

THIS ISN'T ABOUT WATCHING JUST ANY TV show, or just any movie. Or just any video game, if you decide to go that route. It's very specific to your favorites, because this is the "joy" form, and I want to get you through the positive emotion cycle.

The more positive emotions you associate with something, the more likely you are to fully enter the cycle, and get through to security, which will provide the lasting relief we're looking for with Joy Pennies.

When I think of "favorite" TV shows, and favorite movies, I think of either nostalgia or some kind of past association, usually. Would it be your favorite because it reminds you of someone specific? Or of a time when you were at your best, or when life was at its best?

Would it be because of the storyline, or the "tropes" inside the movie? The way it fulfills a desire you have? Or how it reminds you of something very specific?

Whatever "favorite" entails (and you could have multiple favorites), save this card for the favorite. The hit of positive emotions (or maybe the movie that makes you cry, and get out all of your stored-up pain and sorrow) has the best chance of creating a lasting joy.

IF THIS IS A SAVE PENNY:

You will feel relaxed during and afterward.

IF THIS IS A DRAIN PENNY:

You'll feel lethargic after and numb during.

WHERE I SET MINE:

1 cent Save

I only let myself play this card once a day, though, because if I start to use the show to disassociate from life, it loses its power as a Joy Penny. "Not feeling negative emotions because I'm numb" isn't the same as "feeling joy."

Joy Penny 3

Plan your next vacation. Look at the places you'll visit and where you'll stay. Maybe even what you'll eat.

SOME PEOPLE GET A LOT OF ENERGY FROM thinking about the future (especially seeing themselves doing things in the future, like you can experience it in real time, but it hasn't happened yet). When you are wired this way, you will get an almost physical sensation of happiness when you imagine yourself in future happiness.

This is a source of joy pennies many of us forget we have access to, when we need a quick boost of positive emotions. If you're wired this way, you'll experience the future as though it's happening currently. Not like a dream (which is how people whose brains don't function like this will assume you mean), but like it's physically happening to you.

When you know your brain does this, I highly recommend using this as a regular source of joy pennies.

On the flip side, some of us get very stressed out by planning, and it doesn't help us experience joy to think about where we might be going, or to set up options for future trips. In the Joy Pennies, in particular, I am less interested in having you do this exercise if it doesn't bring you joy. I'm more interested in replacing it with something that engages your imagination.

You might look back at past vacations, with pictures, and think about where you've been in the past. You might call a friend or family member and reminisce about where you've been in the past. You might put on that sweatshirt you got at Yellowstone park, or sample that California-made salsa you've been saving, or take a dram of the Irish whiskey you bought in Dublin, or eat Whittaker's chocolate you've been saving from your trip to Christchurch, New Zealand. Whatever engages you in imagination or memory about your travel or your "escape" or your "new and different" experience.

That's what this card is all about.

IF THIS IS A SAVE PENNY:

You will feel excited during and afterward.

. . .

IF THIS IS A DRAIN PENNY:

You'll feel drained (or even stressed) during and/or after.

WHERE I SET MINE:

10 cent Save

Joy Penny 4

Reach out to your favorite person in the world today. Tell them what you appreciate about them. (You can say Becca made you if spontaneous compliments make you uncomfortable.)

I'M AWARE THAT SOME OF US HAVE relational trauma and fear about saying positive things to people. Many of us don't like forced compliments. And if this is something you can't do spontaneously, then I want you to look for a time when you can say something positive to them.

There's a book called "How Full is Your Bucket" (it's actually a Gallup book, so it comes with a Strengths code, which is a happy side note) where the authors talk about how every single interaction you have with someone is either putting a drop in their bucket, or taking a drop out.

(Obviously, I love this, because it aligns with the energy pennies concept, in that every single moment has the potential to do positive or negative work in you. And there is no neutral. Everything has a cost or an add.)

After I read that book, I made an intentional choice to add drops to people's buckets whenever I thought of them. So this particular penny comes easily to me now. But it didn't start off that way. I learned how to do it in a way that wasn't false (because I was genuinely noticing the things as they happened), and I could see the impact it made on my relationships for my friends and family to know how important our connection was. I didn't expect my actions to speak on their own (although I do also expect my actions to speak).

Whether this is a drain or not, I want you to try it and see how you feel. What happens when you notice something and say something positive. (And did you pick the right person to experiment on?)

Set your penny count accordingly, though. If this is too stressful, put a drain on it.

I have a friend whose spouse needs a lot more affirmation than my friend would typically think to give. One of the greatest things about their relationship is that they try to speak love in the way the other person can receive it best (whether you use the "love languages" concept or not, which has been reasonably debunked, but I still think there's value in the underlying concept of giving love the way our partner can receive it). So when my friend realized this about their partner, they decided to start doing bucket drops (without calling them bucket drops) into their partner's bucket regularly. It's been amazing to watch their relationship progress.

But also, I have other friends where this would not go easily or well for them, because their partners don't need the affirmation. So also, not every tool works for every person. Just wanted to acknowledge that. Try it out and see what happens.

Again, make sure it's (1) genuine, and (2) works for your comfort level in regards to timing.

If this is a Save Penny:

You will feel connected, especially afterward. (It might still feel a bit awkward during, especially if you're not used to doing it. But afterward, you should feel connected and secure.)

If this is a Drain Penny:

You'll feel scared before, and likely during, and after, you will feel uncomfortable.

. . .

WHERE I SET MINE:

10 cent Save

Joy Penny 5

Watch the sunrise or the sunset or a rain storm.

INTERESTINGLY, AS I WRITE THIS VERY chapter, the sun is peeking out over the cold, blue horizon. I love the serendipity of this, because I'm actually getting Joy Pennies as I'm writing about Joy Pennies. #sigh

In fact, I specifically bought this house because it has a deck where I can put a table and sit outside with a coffee in the morning, watching the sun. Someday, I will have a house on a lake with a deck where I can do this. Or on a river. That would be the ultimate.

Right now, I can sit at my dining room table, watching the sunrise, and writing this. But if I wanted to get the full penny experience, I'd grab my coffee and go outside.

Unfortunately, it's 12 below zero right now, so that's not happening. But a girl can dream.

I also put "rain storm" here because I want us to be thinking about experiencing the awe of nature on a regular basis. You might want to go to the ocean and watch the surf. You might want to stare out at the snow as it falls. Look at the mountains. Sit under a tree or walk around a botanical garden. Whatever makes you experience awe at this world we have.

So you can customize this card however you'd like, but think about what makes you feel awe when thinking about nature. (If you haven't read the book "Joyful" by Ingrid Fetell Lee before, I highly recommend it. Her definition of joy is slightly different from mine, so you'll find a lot more "happiness" overlap there, which is fine for me. Everyone's definitions are slightly different. But her categorizations of joy were extremely helpful.)

Try it out and see. What happens if you spend some time just staring at the sunrise or sunset or rain storm or blizzard? How do you feel?

IF THIS IS A SAVE PENNY:

You will feel reverent or content during and afterward.

IF THIS IS A DRAIN PENNY:

You'll feel numb or scared or frustrated after.

WHERE I SET MINE:

10 cent Save

Joy Penny 6

Eat something crunchy.

IF YOU'VE EVER BEEN DIAGNOSED WITH AN eating disorder (or if you have a tricky relationship with food), please tread carefully in this chapter, and feel free to skip it.

I know I said Joy and Happiness are not the same thing. But. I did want to include something that was almost purely a "happiness" card.

I would encourage you to make several cards about eating, just because there are also drain cards that relate to eating. (Also acknowledging, I have an eating disorder, so I have to be really intentional around how I think and talk about food, so I won't be talking much about that in this book. Except to say that, even with an eating disorder, as I do more and more work to heal those places that are deep inside that cause some of my behavior, I'm having an easier and easier time in my life talking about food with people.)

But I'm going to make some cards, privately, for myself about the Leaks that I know exist in my eating habits. I'm not going to include them in the game deck, but I'm going to make some suggestions for people here:

* Eating in social situations might be a drain or a leak for some of us.

* Eating sugar might be a drain or a leak.

* Eating flour might be a drain or a leak.

* Eating dairy might be a drain or a leak.

* Eating vegetables might be a drain or a leak.

* Eating meat might be a drain or a leak.

* Eating alone might be a drain or a leak.

Again, hopefully if you're noticing these things in yourself, you're already acting in a self-aware way. But I want to make sure to bring it up because there are a lot of things that can punch holes in our energy penny banks. For me at least, how I eat is a major one.

IF THIS IS A SAVE PENNY:

You will feel happy during and afterward.

· · ·

IF THIS IS A DRAIN PENNY:

You'll feel frustrated or feel nothing. (If we're getting into feeling guilt or shame, that might be a Leak place, and not just a Drain.)

WHERE I SET MINE:

2 cent Save

(and I probably wouldn't play this card every day, because it will lose its interest if it becomes too mundane)

Joy Penny 7
_____

_____

Go to YouTube and find a cat, dog, baby, or other
heartwarming video that will bring you joy.

_____

THIS WAS THE OTHER MAJOR "HAPPINESS"
card in the deck, so I'll say again, for the record,
happiness generally doesn't last. It's not meant to last.
It's meant to be one of the spectrum of emotions we
feel. Trying to be happy all the time (unless you're
wired for it, which does happen) is an exercise in
frustration.

This is why I want us to focus more on the feeling of
contentment or security, rather than thinking of Joy as
being "happy."

But part of the building of that security is by feeling
happy. So here we are. Cat videos. Or dog videos. Or
anything that warms your heart. Honestly, there was

this TikTok trend for awhile where people were mashing up the Quasimodo song with the How to Train Your Dragon song as they showed these amazing vistas, and those videos warm my heart every time.

I also get a heart-warm feeling from watching elite athletes talk about their success process. I get enervated listening to really successful people talk about their mindset. So those would count as this card for me.

A friend recently sent me the Simon Sinek video where he talks about how we need interconnected relationships in order to avoid burnout. It starts off with "you just need one person who believes in you" and I immediately got the heart-warm feeling. So you can get it from a thousand places.

Wherever you find yours, go look for some heartwarming videos to watch. When in doubt, you can start with cats or dogs. But I would encourage you to go looking for the heart-warm moments. In fact, if you search "Simon Sinek One Friend" and you'll find the video I'm referencing. I just double-checked that to make sure.

IF THIS IS A SAVE PENNY:

You will feel heart-warm during and afterward.

IF THIS IS A DRAIN PENNY:

You'll feel frustrated or feel nothing. And if the reason you're feeling drained has to do with forcing yourself to watch videos of something that brings up negative memories, switch to another topic. I lost my companion cat a few years ago, and sometimes I still can't really watch happy cat videos because I miss him so much. Although, even as I say that and I have that hit of internal pain that reminds me of how much I miss him, I also have a huge hit of gratitude for how great he was and how long I had him and how integral he was to my life. So even as I think it might drain me, maybe I'm just assuming. Maybe I need to try it. But the whole point of acknowledging this was to say, if this is a drain for you, switch to a different type of heart-warm videos.

WHERE I SET MINE:

2 cent Save

(For one video… or one set of videos)

CAVEAT: If I get one of these videos at the right time, it's 99 cents for me. When my friend sent me that Simon Sinek video last night, I cried with relief and I could feel all the positive energy pennies. But that's not going to happen every time I watch one of them. So. In the right situation, the number of pennies might change. :)

Joy Penny 8

Drive or walk "the pretty way" to work or the store or the coffee shop. Notice the pretty.

I FEEL LIKE EVERYONE HAS A "PRETTY" WAY and a "fast" way. I'm a scenic route person, so I need to intentionally make myself remember that driving isn't just a utility.

If you don't want to do this on the way to or from the store, do it at another time. Maybe take a whole drive where you just go somewhere that's pretty.

In fact, for me, I don't always go to nature to find the pretty. There's a neighborhood in St. Paul called Summit Hill, and I drive up there a lot because of how gorgeous the houses are and how historic everything is. I often stop and park at this little outlook where you can see the river and all these historic places, and just stand there and take it all in.

I love this place. Clearly.

But you could drive through a beautiful neighborhood with gorgeously appointed houses. You could drive through a Christmas Light neighborhood in December, or you could drive through the cherry blossoms in June. Whatever your definition of pretty is.

My hope is, there would be no "Drain" pennies here, but of course, there might always be a drain to someone. If you are feeling drained by this card because of the driving, try walking instead. Or riding a bike. Whatever gets you to the Save part of the activity.

IF THIS IS A SAVE PENNY:

You will feel heart-warm or in awe during and afterward.

IF THIS IS A DRAIN PENNY:

You'll feel frustrated or feel nothing.

WHERE I SET MINE:

2 cent Save

Joy Penny 9

Name five things you are grateful for. Say them out loud, Miz Mollee, and enunciate.

WHEN WE RAN THE KICKSTARTER FOR THE Energy Pennies deck, you could back at a level where your name would be on one of the cards. I loved the request, when one of our backers (whose name is Molly) asked if she could be Miz Mollee on the card. I giggle every time I read it, so... Joy Penny for me. Thank you, Molly.

I won't belabor all the studies that have been done around gratitude and how much better your day will be just because of gratitude alone. The studies are significant. If you are not currently doing some kind of gratitude practice regularly, hopefully this card will help.

Get some energy pennies from it.

I'm going to set my card pretty high here because while I'm thinking about it, it doesn't seem like a big deal, but after I stopped writing this chapter and went to my journal… I feel so full and so buoyant.

So now I'll say them out loud.

I feel grateful that Molly asked for her nickname in this chapter. I love asking for what you really want. I'm so happy to give people what they really want in earnest, and I love that I got to do that.

I feel grateful for everyone who backed this Kickstarter. It's been a labor of love to get this project off the ground and I genuinely think it has the power to change our lives. I cannot wait to see the effects of it.

I feel grateful that I live in a warm house because it's so cold right now. And the toasty feeling of my soft slippers and my soft sweater make me even more cozy. This is my favorite feeling. It's why I live where the air hurts my face. To get cozy.

I feel grateful that I have friends who check in on me and who care enough to take their time to help me. I am so blessed by their presence in my life.

I feel grateful to live in a place that makes me feel so alive. There's always something to do here, but I also feel totally comfortable staying in my cozy house with my colorful walls and my coffee and my writing and just being happy here. I'm so grateful for St. Paul.

And saying those out loud made me feel even better. I think that might be a 50-cent Joy Penny for me. I still feel the warmth, even ten minutes later. I also feel compelled to share this gratitude with others.

CAVEAT: I am not one of those people who thinks you should say things you're grateful for when you don't actually feel the gratitude. If you don't feel grateful for anything, wait until you do. Don't say things out loud you don't mean, or admit to emotions you don't feel. That's not helpful. What helps us get to the security of Joy is when we feel the feelings we feel. And we can wait to feel them if we don't feel them right now. Not everything is for this moment.

IF THIS IS A SAVE PENNY:

You will feel heart-warm during and afterward.

IF THIS IS A DRAIN PENNY:

You'll feel resentful that you have to do it, and potentially even angry at me for suggesting it. If that's the case, definitely skip this one. I mean, I don't love it when people are mad at me, but I'm more interested in your mental state. :) If this is not for you, it's not for you.

Also, because my copyeditor reminded me that sometimes the "enforced" rules of some families, religions, or educational systems often include an assumption that there's a "right" way to make affirmations work, ignore me.

Like all things, none of this is a "have to," but sometimes there are threat-detector responses internally that have more to do with our background than whether or not a particular suggestion will work for our brains. So ignore me, if that comes up.

WHERE I SET MINE:

50 Cent Save

Joy Penny 10

Clean and/or organize one room in your house or apartment.

HEAR ME OUT, HEAR ME OUT.

I know a lot of us have some level of executive function issues (especially given the overload of our attention, digitally, which I don't think enough of us are acknowledging), so for many of us, this card does not feel like joy. But. Hear me out.

There will be some things in this book that may cost us pennies at first, but will be a net gain in the end, and I want to encourage us (as our executive function allows) to take some action here.

And I'm also going to say, even if we are not the person to clean it or organize it (so whether or not it relies on my personal executive function to complete), I still think this is exceptionally important to our long-term joy.

To the point where I would rather see us paying someone to help us organize rooms in our houses than I would see us doing other things with that money. And I recognize the privilege in that statement. One hundred percent.

I'm also not going to pull punches when it comes to what I have seen work in coaching. I think that's most of the reason anyone listens to me. I have a volume of experience in sitting with people through their pain points and figuring out ways to individually solve their problems.

This is one that I cannot stress enough how important it is to our overall and long term peace.

You may not realize how much a disordered environment is impacting you until you clear it. However. Not all of us will be helped by having forty-five identical plastic containers in our pantry that we have to take cereal out of the box to fill. Some of us will. But that isn't what I mean.

I mean... get your environment to a level of clean and orderly that makes you feel finally at peace. You may not recognize how much a disordered environment is impacting you.

And also, I have to acknowledge that many of us can't afford to hire people, and we may not have the friends or family needed to come in and help us without being paid. For that, I'll say, you're released from this expectation and I hope there's a moment in the future where you're able to do some of this unpacking, cleaning, organizing, moving, or decorating on your own. Because it's a foundational aspect of our productivity (how our environment impacts us).

If it creates a drain on you (energetically) to clean or organize, though, make sure to put the drain pennies on this one. And you're welcome to ignore me, of course. I don't know everyone's life intimately and I don't want to create expectations that will stress you out.

Here's what I will say to those who save Pennies with this. Many of you may already do cleaning and organizing as a "save" activity. (Potentially even doing organizing or cleaning when you're stressed out.) If that's the case, this is a card I would play regularly.

And, when you're finished with the cleaning, and the space is finally either decluttered or organized, sit with that feeling. Let yourself feel how secure it is to have an ordered home. (Again, knowing that not everyone sees "order" in the same way.)

IF THIS IS A SAVE PENNY:

You will feel relieved afterward.

. . .

BECCA SYME

If this is a Drain Penny:

You'll feel frustrated and not want to do it.

Where I set mine:

25 Cent Save

Optional Additional Joy Pennies

I HAVE BEEN COLLECTING SOME ACTIVITIES that I think you might want to consider adding to your joy pennies list, but which I did not include on the printed cards. So here are some thoughts for where you could add other cards to your own deck or list.

- Pet my dog / cuddle with my cat.
- Walk in a field or stroll through a park. (This is specifically different from the Action Pennies suggestion. This strolling card would be more about taking time to enjoy the world around you or to be in full silence mode.)
- Read a book. (A physical book.)
- Have sex.
- Talk to a friend who will let you feel all your feelings.
- Eat your favorite meal.
- Go shopping.
- Get a pedicure, manicure, or massage.

- Play a game with a friend or family member.

Okay, and now notice what things aren't on this list. There is no digital activity on this list. (The favorite TV/Movie one we already have is plenty enough.) There are a lot of things that can be produced by the computer or by digital media or social media.

Peace is not one of them.

I recognize that a lot of us are very tied to our technology and we're very reluctant to admit that the phone might be a source of drains (and even leaks) for us. But I just want to encourage you, if you haven't already, to listen to the Tristan Harris episode of the Trevor Noah podcast. (Be warned, it's intense. But it's a good intense.) It will hopefully provide some reasoning to be less and less connected to technology over time.

PART VI

Courage Pennies

When I think about the different "Forms" of energy represented in the deck, this form was the first one, after Joy, to be really obvious to me. It's hard to describe what I see when I coach people because so much of it is energetic, it's almost physical.

I can physically see it on their face when they come to the relief point. I can physically see the emotions manifest in their body. I can physically see when energy drains or saves in them.

It's weird to talk about because I'm not sure it's something that people would find "normal" but it happens so consistently, I've learned to stop questioning what I'm seeing.

When I see people get Courage Pennies (or lose them), it's almost like I can see a flash of bravery in their features. The thing they're doing takes a hit of courage to face, and when they do the thing, they get a special kind of energy back.

The knowledge that they can do hard things.

I have a friend who was telling me, when I first started describing the "I can do hard things" energy, that this was something he didn't need. But he was ascribing "battlefield" levels of fear to this courage, and let me be clear: the fear for some of us is significant. But too many of us don't know how to recognize the effects of fear on our nervous system.

Many of us only see fear when we see the catalyst for the fear and deem it worthy of being afraid. So we might be afraid of impending economic collapse, or of someone breaking into our house, but we don't see that we are also afraid of sending an email or having a conversation with a person we care about.

Because "being afraid to send an email" doesn't sound like a real thing. And also, because the fear is not conscious. That's how it controls us. It stays under the radar so we can't catch it. (Personally, I believe that's because a lot of the things it programs to are things we should be afraid of on some level, like disintegration, abandonment, etc. But when we initially fear them, they are worth fearing, because they involve our well being. And when they continue to plague us into adulthood, they are not as necessary for the biological purposes they were made in. This is why I suggest a lot of people do parts work, internal family systems therapy. It helps uncover some of these places where fear might be stopping us, but where we might just see "discomfort" or "I don't like doing it," instead of what's really happening, which is that your body believes something is threatening your security.)

Those "battlefield" levels of fear are not what I'm talking about here, for most of us. Although some of us are conscious enough of the fear and its effects, we will actually know it's in control.

Making exceptions for PTSD (and RSD and other forms of disordered behavior around fear responses), and making exceptions for situations that are genuinely triggering of unconscious responses, here's what I know for certain:

Most of us need more practice staring down the proverbial lions that, when they stand at the mouth of the cave, are freezing us. Not actual lions. Don't anyone go climb in a zoo enclosure or go out in search of lions in the wild.

I mean proverbial lions.

Even if you stare down real lions for a living, but you're never honest about your feelings, then being honest about your feelings will take courage. Staring down real lions might not, but staring down a partner who's been hurt by your actions will.

You still need to do it, friendo. But. It will take courage.

And if you stare down real lions for a living, but are never gentle with yourself, then the gentleness is your courage. This is why the individualizing of your Courage Pennies is so important. Because some of us have an easy time making ourselves work hard, or striving. And some of us have an easy time being gentle with ourselves. Then those things don't take courage for us.

But they will for someone else.

In this Form, there will be some things you don't want to do because they don't interest you or they're not hard for you. And if that's the case, I want you to look at your life or ask the people in your life what they think scares you. (I mean, be ready for the answers, though, because... the answers might be triggering.)

If the thing on the card seems "easy," and you find that everything in this form seems easy, I want you to make your own list of things that are hard for you, or that take courage for you. Here are some options:

* not withdrawing when you are feeling hurt or angry

* listening without speaking

* not correcting someone when they're wrong

* having empathy for someone who isn't like you

* changing your mind

* apologizing

* believing someone's assertion without challenging it

* admitting you are wrong about something

* letting someone else be in control

* allowing yourself to fail

* asking for something you need

* taking a day off

* not picking at a person who said something you don't like

* thinking the best of someone who bothers you

* being grateful

* sympathizing with people you think are weak

Those are just a few options. Not all courage looks like a battlefield, especially to people who think they excel at the battlefield. Sometimes courage is being open to being hurt, being vulnerable, being wrong, not being the smartest person in the room, not protecting yourself from people by pulling away.

Everyone's courage looks different.

So if the Courage cards I write don't resonate, make sure you rewrite them for yourself based on the list you've made.

Even small courage pennies, like the ones I've listed here might be good for you, as well. Even if they don't take more than 1 cent of courage. That's also good. We need to build up the energetic reserves so they're there when we need them.

Ok, without further ado, here are the Courage Pennies.

Courage Penny 1

There's an appointment you've been putting off, Kat. Go get your phone and make the appointment now.

WHILE, FOR SOME OF US, DOING EXECUTIVE function tasks is harder than for others, I want to acknowledge that a fair number of people put off non-urgent tasks for reasons that aren't self-sabotage, ADHD, or trauma. And I want to encourage you to try something, when it comes to some of these tasks that you might have a high level of resistance to.

The first is: reframe.

Maybe the fact that you're not making the appointment does actually mean it doesn't need to be made. Someone else told you it needs to be made, but you don't feel the urgency yourself. And sometimes that's okay. The card might be for later.

The second is: re-imagine.

If you really do want to get the task done, even if you have executive function issues, is there something you could imagine differently that would help you to want to do the task? Could you have an easier time making the appointment if you could do it via email instead of phone? Have you checked if that's an option? Could you imagine the task to be easier than you fear?

(This step isn't for everyone, so if you're getting resistance here, that's ok. I just wanted to suggest another option.)

The third is: can someone else do this? Or does it have to be you?

I've started turning over the scheduling of appointments to my assistant because I will put them off for so long. She has my calendar access, she knows my preferences, but I had to release the control of having things happen exactly the way I wanted them if I wasn't able to do the work myself. Does she schedule things when I would rather not have them? Yes. But the other option is I have to sit on hold with the office for twenty minutes in the middle of my work day. I often don't have twenty minutes in the middle of a work day. So it just doesn't get done.

I went through a process this year where I ranked my level of stress around certain activities (like scheduling appointments) and then processed them in relationship to whether or not it was worth the stress, given the potential outcomes. And I had to test the outcomes. It turns out, even when I make the appointment myself, I'm going to resent the time I have to give on the day.

So if I'm not going to resent it any less on the day it happens, then it really doesn't matter when it happens. I don't like having my schedule for work disrupted, tantamount to anything else. So no matter when I get my haircut, I'm going to resent the disruption.

I experimented enough to know how I really felt, and now I don't make my own appointments, unless it requires my medical history (and there's even a form you can sign with your doctor's office that allows someone else to schedule things for you… godsend).

Of course, I recognize that not all of us have someone we can turn those things over to, but many of us do, and we just aren't asking for the help because we need to be in control of everything.

(I'm sorry. But I'm not sorry.)

OKAY, IF YOU'VE DONE ALL THREE OF THOSE things (or what of them you'd like to do or can do), and they haven't worked, then I would likely put this penny as a drain for you.

When it comes to the Courage Pennies, anytime something is a big drain, and we can put it off, I expect it to get put off. It will often become a bigger Drain to put off than it will to accomplish the penny. Let me see if I can explain this.

If I need to make a dentist appointment, and I put it on my list on January 10th, it might cost me 5 pennies of stress in a day to see that on my list and not accomplish it. But then it did cost me 5 drain pennies in that day. At some point, the drain becomes big enough that it causes me to do the thing. (Or at some point, the external pressure becomes enough that I have to do it. Or, if you have executive dysfunction, you don't do it, and then you do it, but you can't always predict when you'll do it.)

So if you're playing the game, and you're getting drain pennies from not completing the task, even if it's a small amount, I would consider adding those to your totals.

Obviously, if you have diagnosed ADHD, this card is going to change for you, and if you haven't heard of Quinn Ward, I recommend giving them a follow on TikTok. I mainly want to see us not throw our hands up in despair of getting things done anytime executive function comes around. We can be creative in the way we support ourselves, and Quinn will be a great resource for ideas there.

I'm also going to say, in case I haven't said it yet... we are all doing too much. So a good portion of our executive overload (when it's not actual dysfunction) is because there's just too much to do.

That's a drain, as well.

Anyway, not for this card. We'll talk about that in other places. But I wanted to bring it up because a lot of us think there's something dysfunctional about us when it's really that we're living in an overstimulated world that expects too much from us because those expectations are rooted in corporate profit, and not in what's best for human beings.

I promise, I'll stop.

IF THIS IS A SAVE PENNY:

You may still dread doing it, but afterward, there will be more relief than there was dread.

IF THIS IS A DRAIN PENNY:

You will resent me for even bringing this up, and you might not even make it to the end of this chapter.

WHERE I SET MINE:

10 cent drain

Because I resent even having to make appointments, to a point where I will actively put them off until I have to have them… and executing the appointment doesn't make me feel any better; I just want the experience of having to be disrupted to go away; can't do that, though, so... that's where I set mine.

Courage Penny 2

Text that person you've been thinking about.

I'll wait here...

OH, PAST BECCA. YOU ARE AWFUL.

Because I've been committing to doing these cards as I write them, and there's a person I've intentionally been putting off texting, I'm a bit mad at Past Becca right now.

I have to choose between continuing to do what I said (complete the cards as I write them) and letting my past trauma win out. Well, apparently the "we can do hard things" motto is really real.

To be completely fair to the content of this card, when I first read it, I was thinking about the different things that require courage, and I completely **repressed** the fact that you have to have conflict sometimes.

Ooof.

Turns out Past Becca was inadvertently smart, because this card can have multiple meanings.

It could mean that person you're new friends with. It could mean that person you haven't seen in a long time. It could mean that person you're newly in love with, or that person you've been dating for awhile. All amazing things. Just a reminder to text them.

But also. It could mean a friend you've had a rupture with. It could mean that friend you're not texting because there's going to be conflict if you do. It could mean a family member you need to have a hard conversation with. It could mean a spouse or partner you've been ignoring because you don't want to be vulnerable.

I don't think I really considered all the ways in which this card could be about conflict, too, which is... on brand for me. This could really be a drain for some of us.

So let's talk about it.

If the person you're thinking about is a friend, lover, partner, and the content of your text will be positive, there might still be resistance there. Some of us fear intimacy and commitment. For really reasonable reasons, by the way, if you understand brain chemistry and how parts of the brain function. Texting someone as a bid for connection might feel really vulnerable to us.

Because what happens if they don't really want to hear from us? What happens if they're mad or done? Wouldn't it be easier if I just didn't reach out? Then they can't reject me?

So there's that kind of courage. The courage of intimacy and connection. The courage of building relationships and being vulnerable.

But if the person you're thinking about is on this side of conflict (where it hasn't happened yet), you might fear the disconnection or the confirmation that they really are mad. Or you fear that they won't respond at all (confirmation that there's no connection there).

Or maybe you have done something wrong and you don't like admitting it. You rushed to judgment. You didn't follow through on a commitment you made. You said something you shouldn't have. You were defensive and mean. You were wrong.

Ouch again.

And then there's the possibility that you're on the other side of conflict (where you've already ruptured) and you fear getting drawn back into that cycle again. (Which, let me just say… if you're in no-contact, this is not an excuse to break no-contact. Text someone else.) You might fear the lead-up to the conflict or triggering a re-engagement.

Only you will know for sure, when the potential contact involves conflict, whether or not you should re-engage. There are reasons to avoid this.

And if the possible outcome could be positive, let me just say... our brains lie to us a lot, trying to keep us inside patterns that were created to keep us safe, but which are no longer necessary. If this resonates with you, I'm going to recommend Sarah Baldwin and Thais Gibson again. There's a good chance you're trying to solve a thinking problem that needs to be solved in the body instead.

Just a thought.

Anyway, when we're talking about courage in the face of things that might be a positive, I want to remind us that our brain can lie to us. So we might be believing outcomes that aren't really going to happen, but which our brain is inventing because it thinks it needs to keep us safe from that potential negative outcome.

Consider texting the person.

We have to experience things in order to learn. And the way we learn to be better at things we're not good at is through experience. We can't book-learn our way into being more courageous.

We have to act and experience our way into courage.

IF THIS IS A SAVE PENNY:

You may still dread doing it, but afterward, there will be more relief than there was dread.

IF THIS IS A DRAIN PENNY:

You will resent me for even bringing this up, and you might not even make it to the end of this chapter.

WHERE I SET MINE:

5 cent save

Courage Penny 3

Say no, Amy.

You can blame Becca if you want, but say no.

TO BE COMPLETELY FAIR, THIS DIRECTIVE CAN
go in two ways, as well. Some of us have a hard time
saying no because we think we can do more than we
can do. That version of "no" is more like, "you can't
write 14 books in a year, Amy," rather than "it's ok to
say no to this person, and they won't hate you" (which
is the other direction this can go).

Some personalities struggle more with the first (excited
by all the opportunities) and some struggle more with
the second, so let's talk about both.

SAYING NO TO POSSIBILITIES

When I have a personality that gets lit up by all the potential things I could do, be, say, experience, then I'm the most likely to struggle with saying no to possibilities. This can be a good thing (in that these types of people also tend to be okay when all the possibilities can't happen, so they're not disappointed in the same way others would be if they want to do something and they can't).

It can also be a detriment, and this tends to happen specifically with commitment.

Saying No To People

As long as we're not pulling punches in the vulnerability department, let's get right in to the "I'm not allowed to say no" trauma that some of us have.

Obviously, if you have been trained in childhood that you're not allowed to say no, you're going to struggle to say no as an adult. It's a surprise to some people that the ways we were trained in childhood still impact us to this day, but they do. And many of the subconscious actions we take were laid down in neural pathways (in our brain's way of thinking, it was "for our benefit," even if the reality of that statement is no longer true) when we were younger.

Decoding or reparenting work is super important to do as an adult, especially when it's inhibiting our ability to function as we want in the world. Anytime you find yourself doing something you don't want to do, assume there is a neural net somewhere misfiring for some reason.

It's possible to heal those spots and retrain those paths. It's just harder work to do than most of us want it to be. (No, it's harder than anyone wants it to be. But some of us are better at doing the work than others.) It's important work, though.

Objectively, when you know what you want to do, but something is keeping you from doing it, *knowing* something else has control of your will is not comfortable. Also, though, that part is doing its best. It thinks it's being helpful.

Again, I encourage parts work / IFS therapy. I also regularly encourage people to read *How to Do The Work* by Nicole LaPera here.

IF THIS IS A SAVE PENNY:

You may still dread doing it, but afterward, there will be more relief than there was dread.

IF THIS IS A DRAIN PENNY:

You will resent me for even bringing this up, and you might not even make it to the end of this chapter.

WHERE I SET MINE:

5 cent Drain

I would have put this at a 99 cent drain a year ago, but I've been doing a lot of work on myself in the area of setting boundaries, so I'm improving... maybe someday, this will be a 99 cent save!

(Oh, my sweet summer child...)

Courage Penny 4

There's a financial task you've been putting off doing. Take the first step today.

UGH. I HAVE BEEN DREADING EVEN WRITING this chapter, specifically because I know I have to do the thing on the card, and I really, really don't want to do anything related to financial tasks.

Clearly, this will be a drain card for me, but I also think it's important to talk about why it's such a drain.

Not just for me (because I'm trying to help provide guidelines for how to do this work), but for everyone.

When I see finances being a drain on people, and when the drain is not directly attributable to "I can't pay my bills this month," it typically comes from a few specific places.

* being underpaid for your work - This is the "if a Big Mac costs 3x what it cost in 2001, why doesn't the McDonald's worker make 3x what they made in 2001" phenomenon. i.e. If the cost of goods goes up, technically labor is also a "good," so all goods should go up commensurately unless the system is being messed with. More and more of us are starting to wake up to the fact that a large part of our financial stress comes from the disparate cost of the things we're buying, compared to the buying power of our working hours. I cannot stress, from an Energy Pennies place, just how big a drain this is, subconsciously, on anyone whose wages are fixed by others. If your boss hasn't compensated for the times, you're going to be under more stress than you would normally be because your subconscious brain can pick up on the fact that you just don't make enough money to afford your life. This alone can make financial tasks stressful, and the worst part is, we don't even know what the stress is. It's helplessness. And it's killing a lot of us.

* childhood wounds representing on current situations - I'm just gonna go here because I'm feeling punchy today. Many of us have a tape that plays in our head as regards the way we expect ourselves not to make mistakes. That tape was most likely laid down in childhood (and sometimes, even in benign circumstances). But it will make us avoid financial tasks because the potential of failure is so significant. (Me doing something wrong, inadvertently or not,

carries a lot of weight internally when I have wounds about fear of failure.)

* brain chemistry - Some of us have unpredictable brain chemistry. Sometimes our executive function works, and sometimes it doesn't. There are ways to manage this (behavior training, body work, medication, etc.), but not everyone has equal access to the resources, so some of us are working against brain chemistry with basically no support at all. Yet we might still be expecting ourselves to be fully functional, and that creates even more stress.

* heightened responsibility - When you don't have a safety net. When your family can't afford to bail you out if this writing career doesn't go well. When you don't have a 401K. When you are responsible for a lot of people's well-being (financially), the worry that your finances aren't going to be enough to sustain the business at some point (it's never immediate, it's always future-oriented), then you're always looking for markers of downturns. This creates hypervigilance and anxiety.

Additionally, for those of you who aren't used to this responsibility level—when you've built a business that suddenly requires this kind of vigilance, but you've never had it before. You're going to experience a drain around finances, even if you're doing well. Whenever you have to pay too much attention to factors you don't usually watch, it creates a disparate energy penny exchange.

Those are only the four biggest. And they all create a pretty significant set of stresses that can keep us from accomplishing even small tasks.

And again, this is not even to touch the stress of, "I can't pay my bills this month," which is also a reasonable stress. And it can't always be alleviated by thinking. (Non-dependable sources of income often create pockets of "flux" and pockets of "lack," so many of us are used to that rhythm. But it's still a stressor.)

So this might not be a card you just blithely say, "I'm gonna do this thing" because putting it in front of you to do and not doing it will only frustrate you more and more.

If this is a big drain for you, but you still want to do it, try some of the grounding techniques that calm your nervous system first. And then try the task. In fact, I know I've recommended the Sarah Baldwin episode on the Mark Groves podcast before, but I'm going to recommend it again if this is resonating too hard.

And after all that, there are those of us who still just put tasks off when there is no pressure attached, so there are all kinds of reasons why we might be putting this off, and not all of them are big. If you are a person who needs pressure to accomplish tasks, try making this the one thing you want to do tomorrow. Get up in the morning and do it right away. See what happens. Make it the first card you play tomorrow. See what happens.

. . .

IF THIS IS A SAVE PENNY:

You may still dread doing it, but afterward, there will be more relief than there was dread.

IF THIS IS A DRAIN PENNY:

You will resent me for even bringing this up, and you might not even make it to the end of this chapter.

WHERE I SET MINE:

50 cent drain - But I'm still gonna do it.

Courage Penny 5

Make that reservation you've been wanting to make, Claire. Or that plane ticket... get it booked.

AND ONCE AGAIN, ANOTHER CARD THAT smacked me in the face, as I've been putting off making flight reservations for a couple of conferences. I guess they say you teach what you most need to hear? Apparently, I need to hear the "play the Courage Pennies game" message this week.

Keep it light, Becca. No punches.

Ok, this one needs less explanation because I don't see a lot of "underlying" reasons here, other than fear of travel and financial stress, and we've covered those already.

But once again, I'll say, it's not uncommon for us to put things off simply because there's no pressure to get it done. But it's often easy to shortcut that (assuming you don't have ADHD, in which case, sometimes your brain is just not predictable) by either gamifying it (rewards can be one way, outside of this game), body-doubling, or making it the morning priority (before the brain has a chance to get too "in the day" yet).

IF THIS IS A SAVE PENNY:

You may still dread doing it, but afterward, there will be more relief than there was dread.

IF THIS IS A DRAIN PENNY:

You will resent me for even bringing this up, and you might not even make it to the end of this chapter.

WHERE I SET MINE:

1 cent Drain

Courage Penny 6

Ask for what you want. Yes, there's a possibility
you won't get it. But you absolutely won't if you
don't ask.

GOOD WORK, PAST BECCA. I NEEDED THIS.

When I first wrote this description in the e-book
version with the print deck (which we released in late
2023), I had included only a dismissive paragraph
about how I wasn't the best person to be discussing
"ask for what you want." My editor had one note in
this micro-chapter.

"Expand. Why not?"

And here's the honest truth. I was working through
some past trauma work related to asking to have my
needs met, and as someone who compulsively meets

the needs of others to prove I'm worthwhile as a person (any other 2/3 Enneagrams?), I couldn't even verbalize the answer to her question.

When she first wrote that note, I thought, "nope, I won't explain that any more. This chapter can stay short."

But almost eight months later, going through her notes with intention, I'm not walking away from this one, because if you're in the same place, you need to know there's hope here.

The two people I suggested checking out (Sarah Baldwin and Thais Gibson) were helpful in my work to overcome some of this. As has been Claire Taylor, in her Enneagram work. But this is a particular sticking point for me.

What I learned about myself: the deepest fear I have was keeping me from the thing I wanted the most. And I see it over and over in people I coach, so I should be familiar enough with it to spot it in myself. My belief that I should be helping others or meeting others' needs has made me less likely to ask for what I want and need.

Ever.

Fundamentally, this was a self-esteem issue (which I rejected at first... insisting that I actually had very healthy self-esteem). And it's been quite a bit of daily work to keep myself emotionally above the line as I heal these places. But I am definitely healing them.

Here's the thing. Our brains lie to us. Not intentionally. They just don't know any better. They internalize lessons from childhood, from before we had logic brains and a developed pre-frontal cortex, that are almost always leading us in the wrong direction.

The lesson I learned as a kid are reasonable for a kid, because the thinking did help in the moment. But they are not true. De-programming those lessons is a lot of work, but it's worthwhile work. Just eight months ago, asking for the tiniest thing I needed was so scary to me, I couldn't get out from underneath an oppressive schedule because I wouldn't say "no" to anyone. I kept expecting everyone else to notice my needs and meet them, instead of standing up for them myself.

(Yeah, just wait for the "Why We Burn Out" chapter on this topic... oh, Becca, my sweet summer child...)

Thankfully, the work works. I'm getting better. I've had some major breakthroughs this year (situations where Past Becca never would have been able to stand up for herself, but where Present Becca is getting there).

So if you need courage to start this work, know it can be amazingly beneficial (even though it is absolutely hard). Worth the work, and worth the pain. The relief I'm able to feel now, because I went through those 75 cent drains, is just unreal. (And really, this was a Leak for me, and I wasn't acknowledging it.)

If this is a Save Penny:

You may still dread doing it, but afterward, there will be more relief than there was dread.

IF THIS IS A DRAIN PENNY:

You will resent me for even bringing this up, and you might not even make it to the end of this chapter.

WHERE I SET MINE:

75 cent drain

Courage Penny 7

Reply to the email you've been not-replying-to. Rip the band-aid off, Ryan.

It won't help to wait.

WE FINALLY GOT TO ONE OF THE COURAGE Pennies that's relatively easy for me (and "relatively" in this energy form… that's still a drain). I tend to leave emails unanswered in my inbox, waiting for my thinking brain to process the answers. But the "ding" of the bread machine being done isn't quite enough to move me back to the inbox, so I end up with all these answered emails sitting in my head.

All I really need is the reminder that I have to respond to these emails, and then it feels so good to get them done.

I recognize, though, a lot of us genuinely dread our inboxes on a regular basis. And some of us have situational dread (when there's something in there that will require conflict or disappointment of others, we might let things pile up).

And because we're also talking sustainable productivity, I want to put in a plug for understanding the futility of inbox zero (or of having your inbox open all the time).

If you never take a break from your emails, or your inbox, I'm going to implore you to please experiment with having a day or two where you are not at all checking. In fact, if you are feeling especially tied to your inbox, that's even more of a reason to experiment.

This is the issue with FOMO. (Fear of Missing Out)

If we're afraid of something (especially the "what might happen if I miss this" fear), there is no way to solve that fear without either giving in all the time and trying to never miss out, or experimenting with missing out to see if I'm right. We can't prove a negative to our fear-addicted brains.

We can only prove it will be ok to miss out on things by actually missing out on things.

And if you haven't yet read *4000 Weeks* to really understand the concept of missing out, it might be a worthwhile read.

But if this is a benign courage-need for you, and not a big drain, I would encourage you do use this card as the impetus to open the inbox.

Some of us really struggle to make ourselves do things we don't want to do. (This will sound like crazy talk to some of you, but it's a genuine personality trait.) When we're not as good at it, I do think it's wise to consider practicing this trait. Even when it's not strong for us. (There's a difference between "I'll never be great at it" and "I'll never need it.") I may not be great at making myself do things I don't want to do, but I need to be better than I am. (Basically.)

Again, not all of us are in this place, and if you're "wondering" if this is you, it's not. If you have to wonder, it's not you. :)

IF THIS IS A SAVE PENNY:

You may still dread doing it, but afterward, there will be more relief than there was dread.

IF THIS IS A DRAIN PENNY:

You will resent me for even bringing this up, and you might not even make it to the end of this chapter.

WHERE I SET MINE:

2 cent Drain

Courage Penny 8

The change you've been thinking of making...
start today. Not tomorrow. Try starting today and
see what happens.

You'll see a pattern forming in the
Courage Form, where we're intimately discussing
experimentation. As I said in the last chapter, you can't
prove an absence to your brain. You can't prove a
negative.

If you worry "what happens if I miss out" but you
never miss out, you'll always be captive to that fear.
Always.

In a similar way, when we take action on something we
know will be painful (starting a different way of living,
taking a chance on a new way of life, being engaged in

deeper work, etc.), we are missing out on the old comfort we were feeling when we kept the old pattern.

A couple of years ago, I moved from Montana to Minnesota, and I had to move quite quickly, or I would never move. I had been wanting to make this move for so long (more than a decade), but I'd let the comfort of my old home keep me there.

When I finally decided it might be time, and I got here and realized I had the ability to break out of that comfort, I had to make a commitment very quickly. I rented an apartment in one day and moved in that night, and never went back to Montana.

I still haven't been back. (Two years later, I still haven't.)

The comfort of the old was so sincere. I had 25 years of roots in that town and 43 years of roots in the state. Friends who had known me my whole adult life. I knew that valley better than the back of my hand.

It wasn't serving me, though. It hadn't been serving me for a long time and I didn't see it. In fact, I started traveling hard core the last three years I lived there, and didn't realize how much I was trying to get away from that place.

Not until I got out did I realize how much I'd needed to leave.

So many of us fear change because it's the unknown, and the known is so comfortable. (Also, biologically, our brains are wired not to change... they're wired to keep giving us the same thing they've always given us.) Comfort can feel really good.

Unless it's the heat turning up on the stove and we don't realize it until we're cooked.

That's the reason I put this card in the deck. It takes courage to change, and for some of us, it takes 9999 Drain Pennies to change, because the unknown is so scary. (You may not be in touch with your fear consciously, so you might just think you're hesitant... but it's fear. It's a biological imperative for you to feel fear at change.)

Plus, some of us are great at changing things we want to change, but awful at changing things we don't-want-to-but-need-to-change.

And there are all kinds of other things that might stand in the way of those changes.

But if you haven't heard me talk about the Mississippi River before, I think it's important to put this here.

The patterns in our brains are hard-wired to give us the same of what we've gotten. It's how we survive as a species. You train me how to be, I learn from my environment, and then I keep re-presenting those patterns to keep myself alive until I eventually die.

That's how the brain functions at its best. When it learns the right patterns young, and can just re-present those patterns it's hard-wired through your lifetime.

But when your environment teaches you the wrong lesson, and you assimilate it as though it's the right lesson, you've made the equivalent of the Mississippi River in your head, to keep presenting you with that same behavior pattern.

Here's just one for-instance: going on Facebook as soon as I pick up my phone in the morning. There's an internal cue somewhere that, when I see my phone, first thing in the morning, I want to check in on how everyone's doing. It might have come from a good place, initially, but now it's just an addiction to the closing of the dopamine loop. I might even still consciously think, "I want to see my friends," but what's really happening is that your brain wants the good chemicals. So it'll tell you, "let's really quick check on everyone, and then you can write."

That "really quick" thought is a deep pattern, and if we don't disrupt it, it's going to keep flowing, every time. Then every time you see the phone, you'll want to check in on everyone. And every time you gratify the impulse, the river gets deeper.

And you'll keep re-presenting it until you move the river.

Moving the river is hard work, and it can't be done in a day. And you'll do weeks, months, and sometimes years of work on a particular pattern, only to have it keep flowing as it has always flowed sometimes.

Instead of seeing that as failure, we see it as progress. Of course the river wants to go back to the way it's always flowed. Water's gonna water. It wants to take the easiest route to its gravitational destination, and the old path is the easiest (most well-traveled) route.

Moving the river is a lot. It takes commitment, and it takes a reluctance to give up on the work. Otherwise, we'll keep getting the results we've always gotten.

And for some of us, in some areas, that's not a bad thing, it's just how it is. But when you really do decide you want to change the river, you've got to understand the process you're engaged in so you don't get results that make you want to quit (like the river going back, or appearing to get more aggressive in executing its pattern).

Moving the river is worth it.

Anyway. I know this is a lot for one chapter, and I'll stop now. But I wanted to just say... staying in the old pattern, if it's not what you long-term want for yourself, isn't going to get easier to change, it's going to get harder to change.

If this is the crack you need to commit to the work, I hope it's done its job.

If this is a Save Penny:

You may still dread doing it, but afterward, there will be more relief than there was dread.

. . .

IF THIS IS A DRAIN PENNY:

You will resent me for even bringing this up, and you might not even make it to the end of this chapter.

WHERE I SET MINE:

75 cent Drain

I still resist major changes, and when I make one, it takes a lot out of me. But I know they're important, and I try to take care of myself when I can, and ask for what I need on those days when I need to do something big.

Courage Penny 9

Do something that makes you feel competent. Preferably the most competent you feel, but I'll take "very" competent.

MANY OF US HAVE AN UNCONSCIOUS OR subconscious desire to be competent at things, and when we do too many things that make us feel incompetent (whether we realize it or not), we can end up drained. Doing something that makes me feel competent re-sets that baseline of "I can do things well" that life can destabilize at times.

Not to mention the fact that when we get dysregulated, we need to bring our competent self back online because we've momentarily gotten caught up in the old tapes that make us afraid we're not up to the task at hand. Or that we'll never be up to any task at any point in the future. Or any version of that thinking.

My goal with this card is to encourage the competent self as often as possible. I know we can only do cards once a day to count them, but this is an activity I do regularly when I'm starting to feel the slide down into the "yuck" states, emotionally.

I find that coaching re-sets this for me, when I'm handling a really complicated or complex problem. Playing the piano or singing (which I've been doing professionally on and off my whole adult life). Even things like cleaning (which does make me feel competent, even though I don't like it) and organizing can get me this level of security in my own capacity.

The key is, you won't always think, consciously, that you're incompetent when you need this. Sometimes, you'll just be getting mad at yourself or you'll be frustrated that a thing won't work, or you'll be overwhelmed. You don't always realize this is the thing you need. It's why I want some of these activities to just become regular or rote for us.

IF THIS IS A SAVE PENNY:

You should enjoy doing this activity, although at times, it may feel like a waste of time because it doesn't directly seem to solve a problem.

. . .

IF THIS IS A DRAIN PENNY:

You will think this is a waste of your time, or it will frustrate you.

WHERE I SET MINE:

5 cent save

Courage Penny 10

The person you met that you've been wanting to be closer to... reach out to them with a question or an ask for help.

THIS WAS A SUGGESTION FROM ONE OF THE "beta" readers of this card deck, because I'd originally had the "text someone you're thinking of" card twice, and she made the point that there's really two parts to the "text someone you're thinking of."

There's the person you know and love and are close to (which is the one we already did), and then there's the new friend.

I'm a person who generally believes that most people want to be helpful (and I'm sure that's a bias of mine), but what I've often found is that people have an easier time offering help than making small talk. So when I start making friends, the easiest friendships come when I ask them for help. That's why I put "ask them for help" on the card.

But this is one where you might want to modify that action for yourself. What is a benign action that will give you the option to connect without feeling like it's not you?

And once again, if this is a struggle area for you, I'm going to suggest Thais Gibson's work on attachment styles, just in case you need more guidance there.

But if this is just a harmless action threshold (i.e. I will eventually do this, but there's some resistance to doing it right now), then it might be worthwhile doing the thing and seeing what happens.

IF THIS IS A SAVE PENNY:

You may still dread doing it, but afterward, there will be more relief than there was dread.

IF THIS IS A DRAIN PENNY:

You will resent me for even bringing this up, and you might not even make it to the end of this chapter.

WHERE I SET MINE:

1 cent save

Courage Penny 11

That scary project you've been thinking about but not working on... it's time to face that project. It's not going away until you finish it.

I FEEL LIKE THIS CARD DOESN'T NEED MUCH explanation from me, so I'm going to leave it. If you struggle with this, you've heard everything anyone has to say about it because you've been trying to fix this part of yourself for a long time. (Or, of course, you've been not talking about it or ignoring it because it's scary to think about.) And if you don't struggle with it, you're skimming anyway, so... we're ok to skip the long explanation on this one.

Just know, so often, the major issue we have is the starting of the project. That has the highest threshold. Take one step, and see if it helps. Just do the first part and see if it gets any easier. (It might not, and that's ok. But just see if it does.)

And if this project happens to be a manuscript, try watching my "Stuck List" videos on the Quitcast (it's on YouTube). I go through how to help yourself get unstuck regularly, and they're free.

IF THIS IS A SAVE PENNY:

You may still dread doing it, but afterward, there will be more relief than there was dread.

IF THIS IS A DRAIN PENNY:

You will be frustrated or scared of the outcome. But it can still be a good thing. (If you resent me, this might be a Leak, and then we might be in a different place.)

WHERE I SET MINE:

2 cent Drain

It's still going to drain my energy to start this, even though I know I want to do it and even though I know it's going to feel better when it's done. Sometimes we need to remember that drains aren't always a bad thing.

Courage Penny 12

Don't reach for the phone when you wake up in
the morning.

IF YOU'VE BEEN AROUND THE BFA (BETTER-
Faster Academy) for any length of time, you've heard
me preach this. Over and over.

And I'm going to say it again.

A lot of us are not curbing the use of our phones
because we're afraid of what happens if we don't have
them. And we need to increase our courage in this
arena to become less and less connected to our phones.

Yes, it might be painful at first (the first time I started
doing this, I had a 99 cent drain on this particular
action... it was so hard).

But honestly, when I realize that I'm reaching for my phone again first thing, I get really excited that I noticed it because now I can make myself stop, and I will get the 99 cent energy save back.

Because at this point, when I don't reach for my phone first thing, and when I don't get on social media or in email first thing, I have significantly better days.

Exponentially better days.

And I can see it in hindsight because I've done the experiment. So I'm going to encourage you to also do the experiment if you never have. (And if you don't reach for your phone already, it may not be as big of an energy save for you, because you're already getting it.)

Here's hoping, for some of us, this will help us be less overwhelmed and burned out, and less stressed overall. Even if it's a bit more stressful at first. Worth it.

IF THIS IS A SAVE PENNY:

You may still dread doing it, but afterward, there will be more relief than there was dread.

IF THIS IS A DRAIN PENNY:

You will resent me for even bringing this up, and you might not even make it to the end of this chapter.

. . .

WHERE I SET MINE:

99 cent save

Optional Additional Courage Pennies

I HAVE BEEN COLLECTING SOME ACTIVITIES that I think you might want to consider adding to your courage pennies list, but which I did not include on the printed cards. So here are some thoughts for where you could add other cards to your own deck.

- Compliment someone
- Say no
- Speak in public
- Hit "publish" on your manuscript
- Go to a conference
- Quit your job
- Tell that person how you feel
- Apologize
- Write the next sentence in the manuscript
- End a relationship
- Have a conflict
- Create a course out of your expertise
- Open a business

- Ask for help
- Get a part-time job
- Move
- Tell someone you love them
- Take a vacation
- Hire someone to help you in your business
- Oh... and Ask. For. Help. Jason.

Obviously, some of these are really big Courage Pennies moments. What I'm not suggesting is that you should blithely take any of these things on. But I am suggesting that we need to think about what they require of us.

When something requires courage, and it's a big drain on that courage, we may just not have the pennies to accomplish it. We may not have the bandwidth to open a business right now because of all the other pressures of life (even if we really want to do it). And that might actually be our best life right now.

This is the other thing I need to make sure to hit home again: Just because it takes courage doesn't mean we should feel bad if we're not doing it. Courage isn't righteous. It's just one of the forms of energy we need to get used to expending.

No one's life should be all courage, or they will be completely out of balance. (And you can see some people who are really out of balance, in their upper limit, where life is requiring courage of them at all times. They will absolutely burn out.)

It's a great reminder to bring us back to the fact that a good life requires all six types of energy.

All six.

So maybe we just do one courage card a day. And maybe we make some small courage cards (like complimenting someone or shutting down the computer).

Make Your Own List Or Cards

WHILE WE AREN'T CURRENTLY SELLING THIS game anywhere, you can make your own version of it. You can either print the cards or design them yourself, or you can make lists of the activities for the day, and have a ready plan for when you need to balance your energy.

If we ever do sell the game at any point in the future, it will be listed on our merch store: http://betterfasteracademy.com

But for now, we have no plans to sell this game. It was a Kickstarter Exclusive from 2023 and we likely won't print or distribute it unless something massively changes in the business.

We've given suggestions for how to reverse engineer the game in several places, and hopefully that will help. You're more than welcome to make your own physical cards if you'd like. My goal is just to see people use some kind of gamified support in their energy management. We need to make this in/out dynamic sustainable.

And having fun is the easiest way to do it.

SIX

What It Looks Like to Play This Game

I WANT TO GIVE YOU SOME PRACTICAL application of what it might look like to play this game.

HIGH VIGILANCE

You go through all the pennies and make notes for yourself about what actions belong in the forms of energy, for you.

You have lists for either each form (if you like to make sure to get all the forms in one day, or one week), or you have lists for each denomination of currency.

You have a piece of paper with the day's totals or the day's activities, and you play the game with the denominations, trying to get your $1 for the day so you "win" the game. Or your $2 for the day.

You count the negative/drain cards in addition to the positive ones.

. . .

Focusing on the Save Cards (for High/Mid)

You make lists of all the things that "save" you energy, and you try to play those regularly. You may make lists for the day or the week or month. There may be a habit tracker or task wheel involved, but it's going to be likely you'll refer back to the book on occasion, or make some lists for yourself.

Mid Vigilance

You do something from one of the cards that's feels big (say, Courage Penny 8 about big changes starting today), and it's a huge drain on you. To compensate, you spend the day doing Joy, Spirit, Thought, and Rest Pennies that fill your tank.

You may play from the list. You may not.

You may have some idea of tasks being "bigger" or "smaller" in denomination than others. You may not.

But you consciously use some part of the game (the forms are the easiest part... getting a diversity of forms in your day when you have to do something big that's draining). Maybe not on a daily basis.

The primary way I want to see you focus on using these cards is to intentionally fill the well when you know you've done something draining.

Ask for what you need (time, space, resources, attention) when you know you've had a big drain. Make the Save Pennies.

Additional Gamification (High/Mid/Low)

You may make a Bingo Card to gamify the process of completing Drains or Saves more consistently.

And if you go to betterfasteracademy.com/epresources you can find a bingo card and other downloadable resources we've made to help you with the game if you want it.

You don't need them. But if you want them, they're there for you.

Focusing on the Drain Cards (for High/Mid)

You make lists of all the things that "drain" energy from you, and you try to track when those are happening. You may make lists for the day or the week.

When you notice you're doing a lot of "drain" activities, you intentionally try to do some "save" activities. And those might be the days you decide to try to hit $1.

. . .

Low Vigilance and Those Who Have Played The Game A Lot

By now, I don't need to track my pennies anymore. I've been doing this for so many years, and I'm so conscious now of what level of drain or save something is for me, I have developed a bit lower of vigilance over time.

It did take time, because I'm a naturally high vigilance person, but I did get to the place more like the Low Vigilance people. Here's how I imagine a lot of Low Vigilance people will act.

You may come back to this book once in awhile, just as a list. But the likelihood is, you've got an intuitive sense for what drains you and what doesn't, and you naturally use that in/out flux.

Where you need to start paying attention is when you really get drained and you're not sure why. That's a good time to take a cycle through the Courage Pennies or Action Pennies and see what might be causing the problem.

Essentially, this book can help as a diagnostic tool for when your intuition knows there's something wrong, but you can't quite figure out what it is.

You may flip through the lists in the middle of the book occasionally (and you might read them through the first time, just to see how each action might impact your subconscious. (Because I talk about that in each penny chapter.)

But you probably won't ever use the numbers or keep any lists. This is just a tool for assimilating thinking.

HOWEVER YOU USE THE GAME IS VALID.

SEVEN

Burnout's Impact on Energy Management

In the untouched Alaskan wilderness, blue ice floats in the water like the dregs of crushed ice in a slushee. But beneath the surface, a vast and dense block of ice hides below that little peak. Some bigger than others, obviously—the bigger the peak, the vaster the block.

But when you ride through the iceberg castoffs, those dense blue blocks have Titanic echoes. Especially when you're also in a big ship. Anyone's mind might go there.

The purpose of that imagination—that moment when you flash to the Titanic hitting the iceberg—biologically —is to serve as a warning sign. It's like the flash in your mind of falling down the stairs when you're walking around stairs. Your mind is reminding you to be careful.

There are always signs for caution.

If you've ever burned out before, when you start to over-work, your mind will do a similar thing, flashing to the image of you unable to move on the bathroom floor, as a warning sign. Or flashing to the moment you checked your book sales and they were free falling because you hadn't published in a year.

But I want to say, very clearly, this is not a book about burnout. It's a book about sustainability. Finding the the magic in our lives again, and learning to ignore the Titanic flash that happens when we fear entering "normal" status after burning out.

Like a lot of games, the Energy Pennies Game we're about to discuss is meant to provide structure, incentives, and motivation to participate.

The reason I wanted to gamify the process of energy management is exactly this Titanic flash. So many of us have been warned, so often, about the dangers of overworking or of burnout. It's making us fear self-care (because that disrupts the work) and it's making others of us fear work (because we don't want to "go back there" again).

Gamifying energy management means you won't go too far. You won't "only" do things you like. You won't "only" do things that are too easy or too hard.

For some of us, we need the reminders to practice self-care at all. To disrupt the work and take care of our systems.

For others, we need the reminders that we only have to do what the game requires of us. We only need 100 pennies to win a day.

(And there are some activities that are 99 pennies. So. It doesn't take a ton of effort to keep sustainably managing our energy.)

However you're coming to this book, I hope it will provide a helpful guideline for either burnout recovery, overwhelm management, or fun-seeking.

Many of us need more fun-seeking in our lives anyway.

We have had too much stress. Or too much work. Or too much worry. And we need some "balance" (which is a charged word... we're not talking about"work-life balance" here... just the concept of "not too much of one thing, not to little of its opposite").

My father is a farmer, and something I've learned well about appropriate resource management is that you need fallow time, and then you need hard work. Even the land needs to rest.

EIGHT

Why We Burn Out

THIS IS THE CHAPTER I DON'T WANT TO write. In fact, it's the last chapter I'm writing, in the chronology of writing... the rest of the book is done and edited, and I've been avoiding this blank page long enough, I have to kick in and get it done.

In the very beginning of the book, I alluded to the fact that I had to cancel Christmas with my family in order to recover from burnout, but the reality is, I'm recovering still from all the burnouts of the last decade. Still.

I never really recovered.

Because I never fixed the source of my burnout.

The systemic reason I keep burning out is that I've built a business that functions on my time. The only way my business makes money is if I sell my time. And that time can only get sold once.

As beneficial as the coaching time might be to an individual person, I can't charge enough money to compensate for the fact that my time is the commodity. That wouldn't be reasonable to my clients.

I've already had to do two price jumps in the last two years, just to make sure the people who need to see me really need to see me. But even in that case, I still need to build a part of my business that doesn't function because I'm putting time into it.

I need to build some content infrastructure that makes money without me, because I need the infrastructure to keep running the business when I desperately need time off.

But in order to make that content arm of the business, I have to spend more of my time, when I'm still burned out. And it's been rough.

I'll retract just enough, every eight months or so, to get another burst of energy, that I subsequently spend making the business function.

(Also, any of you who are clients who are reading this, no guilt to be felt on your part. I coach willingly and love it. It just can't sustain a business the size it takes to run mine. I need some things that don't require my immediate time, in order to allow for me to have time off from the coaching. This is not the clients' fault. I love helping my clients and students. This is my fault.)

Over the last two weeks, I've been going through a deconstruction of my expectations around what I'm able to do myself. I had to bring on a COO to manage my operations. I had to take a risk in hiring this person because I believe there's efficiency that could be gained in me turning everything over.

But I'm the one who's been making this business function for ten years. I keep just adding things onto my plate and eating into my personal time to get my work done. I have been in the cycle of, "every time the business needs money, I can open my calendar more," and that's been *fine*, but not *good*, if you know what I mean.

I ended the last chapter with "Even The Land Needs Rest," and I almost titled this chapter with that sentence.

Having grown up around the rhythm of planting and harvest, I've seen how natural rhythm can be sustainable. The land we farm has been producing food for hundreds of years. Sustainably. But if I try to get too much from that land, it's not sustainable.

If I don't give it the rest it needs, it won't sustain the food production.

We are also made of the same organic matter. We are alive. There is a rhythm to how our needs and resources need to be cared for.

When we don't honor the organic matter of our own personal system, burnout will happen. We can stave it off, do a patched-up recovery, and keep surviving, of course. But at some point, that cycle becomes unsustainable.

I reached that breaking point this winter. I needed to make a very hard decision and face my fear about this business and about myself in order to do the hard thing. In order to see if this business can make it.

There's a scene in the *Voyage of the Dawn Treader* that I reference a lot in transformative work (which is what I do). It's the scene where Eustace has become a dragon, and he wants to be a real boy again.

So he comes to the pool, where he knows he has to peel off his dragon skin, and he does the tough work, peeling it off. But he wakes up a dragon again.

He hasn't gone deep enough.

When he lets the lion, Aslan, do the work, it hurts more. It goes deeper, and it takes the skin all the way to the bone.

But he wakes up a real boy.

Too many of us, in our burnout recovery, are peeling off our own dragon skin, but not letting the process or the truth about sustainability go all the way to the bone. We don't like the pain that would require. We just want to change what we can change.

We'll do a few things (maybe paint the walls, maybe move across the country), but we won't do the Important Things. We won't get a part-time job to sustain our writing. We won't have the hard conversation with our partner. We won't cut our budget. We won't change careers. We won't leave the marriage. We won't make a commitment. We won't go to therapy. We won't open ourselves to possible pain. We won't be vulnerable. We won't stop eating sugar. We won't cut off that family member. We won't end that business partnership.

But we have to let the process (or someone outside ourselves) peel us down to the bone, if we want the peace of being in our true form. In our organic, whole, sustainable form. Free from the fear of what might happen if we fail or what might happen if we do it wrong or what might happen if we can't do this.

We will continue to burn out, over and over again, if we don't build a sustainable life for ourselves. Sometimes, that requires the really hard choices. But it can prevent burnout in the long run.

And honestly, the relief of being out of the clutches of that fear is so significant, I can't describe it. Yes, it's going to be hard and probably awful. But knowing the peace is coming… it's indescribable.

NINE

Build The House You Want To Live In

WHEN I MOVED INTO THE HOUSE I CURRENTLY own, there was work to be done. The previous owner had set up their office in a way that did not at all benefit my business. There were large, clunky built-ins that needed to go. The walls were all eggshell white.

I had work to do.

Organizing that work took quite a long time. It was a full year after purchase before the house looked like what it does today. The process was long and laborious.

And there's still work to be done. Remodeling to do. Things to tear out. Things to paint over. Things to knock through.

It's going to cost money, so I need to save that money. And it's going to take time, so I have to set my expectations for resilience. It will be disruptive to the current patterns, so I want to plan it in a time it won't derail important projects.

But these are all decisions I wouldn't have made before. Before, I would have just seen the problem, decided the problem needed to be fixed, and then started work. Without thinking about the tax on my systems. Without thinking of the stress.

I don't want to live that life anymore.

This game is just one part of building a sustainable life. There are other parts—and they all involve some kind of remodel. So I'm going to encourage you to consider building a house you want to live in.

Knock some walls down.

Save some money.

Make some hard choices.

If you need support, you know where we are. You know who I am. And you know I've been there.

The last thing I want for any of you is that you'd feel trapped in the life you're living. And while I can't be your personal support, for each and every person reading this book, I can be an encouragement, and I can point you in the direction of resources.

We also do a newsletter column, at least once a month, where I answer letters for subscribers, to the whole newsletter. I have a plethora of free resources on the Quitcast YouTube channel. And I've encouraged you in these chapters with several places to go for help. You're welcome to submit a question. We do free Live Public

Coaching on our Crowdcast channel every month, just so you can ask questions if you can't afford coaching.

Whatever support we can provide, we will.

But so many of us just need the reminder to keep building and keep working and keep remodeling. The work is worth it.

If you could seen into the future, where the house is more peaceful and more secure, and see past all the trial and pain and disappointment, see past all the failures and all the frustrations, and see just how deep and abiding the peace is when you're not being driven by the fear.

You would see: the house you want to live in is worth building. Even when it might take some pain and some time to get there.

It means giving yourself energy (Save Pennies) along the way, and building that emotional resilience that will help sustain the work. It means doing the hard things (Drain Pennies) and then giving yourself the grace you need to recover.

But the house is beautiful, and it's finished, and it's in the future. Now, we just have to make that future happen.

Here's a hammer. Who's with me?

About the Author

Becca Syme holds a master's degree in transformational leadership and has been a success coach (primarily utilizing the Gallup Strengthsfinder®) for over eighteen years. She's coached more than 6,000 individuals, authors, and creatives through her *Write Better-Faster* and *Strengths for Writers* classes & coaching cohorts: six- and seven-figure authors, major award winners, midlisters, and new authors alike. Becca is the host of the YouTube QuitCast for Writers channel and a mystery author.

betterfasteracademy.com

Also by Becca Syme

QuitBooks for Writers

Dear Writer, You Need to Quit

Dear Writer, Are You In Burnout?

Dear Writer, You're Doing It Wrong

Dear Writer, Are You In Writer's Block?

Dear Writer, You're Doing It Right

Dear Writer, Are You Intuitive?

Coming in 2025: Dear Writer, You STILL Need to Quit

———

Better-Faster Author Success

The Author Stuck List

Energy Management for Writers

Coming in 2025: Unwritten Rules for Intuitive Writers

Acknowledgments

FIRST OFF, TO THE KICKSTARTER BACKERS WHO believed in this project so much, you put your money behind it. I'm eternally grateful. Specifically, I want to thank: Amity T., Barbara C., Clare Sager, Dakota Willink, Jenn Falls, Katy K., Kristin S., Lisa R., Marianne, Mia, and Staci L. Y'all are superstars, and thank you for your support.

I have a few friends who really played the "village" that raised this book, and I want to thank them up front. Krystal, Claire, Jill, Stef, Dan... I for sure couldn't have done this without you.

Additionally, I want to thank my friend Jenn for being the person who consistently talks about The Work with me and is always sending me new resources. I love the fact that there's always more to learn about developing ourselves and about nervous system regulation and attachment. Always so grateful for fellow learning-obsessed people who befriend me. I could keep learning about these things forever and never feel like I reach the end.

Even though you'll probably never read this, I want to thank Ruth for being exactly the right friend at exactly the right time for the burnout and overwhelm I've felt for the last year. It's ironic to be teaching and writing about burnout, but to be going through it so aggressively. Ironic might even be the wrong word. But I'm so grateful that you were the right friend at the right time. It helped me so much.

To Geoff, Rich, Paul, and Daniel who, at different times, have provided support for me in ways you may never understand. I certainly can't explain it. I have tried. But to you all, I am grateful. This book wouldn't be done without your very different and very important support, lessons, and companionship at different points over the last two years I've been working on this project. Thank you.

Thank you to my Patreon community, who lets me release random chapters of this stuff and sometimes not see the final product for actual years… you are with me in a way I feel with each word. Thank you.

The entire BFA staff… You know how important you are to me and to the work we do here. Thank you.

To all the writers I've coached and all the students who have come through the BFA classes: thank you.

To the Kickstarter backers who showed an interest in this, even before it was a real thing: Thank you so much for making me feel like there's support for this book.

To God and to my family, I am eternally grateful.

And to you, dear reader—dear writer—I am grateful you're here reading this book with me, and that you've made it this far. Our work here is finished, but our work "there" (where you are, where I am) has just begun.

Let's get to it.

<3 Becca <3

Notes

5. Defining the Terms and Notes Before We Begin The Game

1. For my own hyper vigilance, I would designate each of these as different levels, though. Eating a piece of fruit might be 2 pennies for me because I know it also keeps me from eating table sugar when I have a sweet piece of fruit, and that feels like an added bonus. Missing traffic means I get more time at home, so that might be five cents plus for me.

Action Penny 4

1. There's a whole long story where I got water poisoning at the beginning of the pandemic because someone said to make sure to hydrate to protect yourself from Covid, and sure enough, I drank way too much water and unbalanced my electrolytes.

V. Joy Pennies

1. Please read *The Pathway* or *Wired for Joy* by Laurel Mellin if you want more information about this. I first learned this from her work in the early 2000s, where my therapist was a trained practitioner of EBT, which is Laurel's program. So I haven't learned this from books, but I did learn it from therapy. So I highly recommend checking out those books.